ROAD TO WORK

Succeeding on the Job

New Readers Press
ProLiteracy's publishing division

Ronna Mag

Series Consu
Lia Conklin

Dedication and Acknowledgments

This book is dedicated to those who study and work.

Special thanks to the workers who allowed me to tell their stories in Succeeding on the Job: Eddie Wong, Sergio, Scott Aronchick, Joy Nesem Mergen, Elizabeth Madero, Pierre Giammattei, Zenie Michael, Rafael Contreras, Janna Ramos, Juan Sanchez, and Annie Chin.

Thanks also to the educators and friends who helped me get in touch with the workers: Barbara Hughes, Donna Price, Lia Lerner, and Michelle McCarthy.

—Ronna Magy

Road to Work: Succeeding on the Job
ISBN 978-1-56420-187-4

Copyright © 2017 New Readers Press
New Readers Press
ProLiteracy's Publishing Division
104 Marcellus Street, Syracuse, New York 13204
www.newreaderspress.com

Printed in the United States of America
10 9 8 7 6 5 4 3 2 1

⌐ds from the sale of New Readers Press materials support professional
       ⌐nt, training, and technical assistance programs of ProLiteracy
              ⌐al literacy programs in the U.S. and around the globe.

            ⌐rrie Lipke

            ⌐ryellen Casey

Contents

SCOPE AND SEQUENCE

Unit, Title, Pages	Theme	Career Clusters and Occupations	Language Functions	College and Career Readiness Skills	Informational Text	Critical Thinking, Problem Solving, and Paraphrasing
Unit 1 Providing **Patient Care** Pages 14–19	• Health care • Health related skills • Patient care	Health sciences: nursing • CNA • Personal care assistant	• Talk about health care occupations • Discuss taking career education classes • Make small talk • Discuss the language of patient care	• Read closely • Respond to text-dependent questions • Cite evidence • Build vocabulary • Summarize information • Write about a job you are looking for and the English skills, education, and training needed to get that job	• Read a patient's medical chart	• Solve problems • Paraphrasing
Unit 2 **The Customer is Always Right** Pages 20–25	• Customer service • Communication between employer and employee	Hospitality: restaurant • Chef • Server • Restaurant manager	• Talk about restaurant customer service • Interpret effective customer service language • Talk to a boss • Talk about customer complaints	• Read closely • Respond to text-dependent questions • Cite evidence • Build vocabulary • Retell a story • Write about good customer service	• Read tips for good customer service	• Critical thinking: draw conclusions • Paraphrasing
Unit 3 **Be Healthy and Safe at Work** Pages 26–31	• Workplace safety: repetitive stress injury • Communication between employer and employee	Sales: supermarket • Cashier • Stock clerk • Store manager	• Talk about working conditions • Report a workplace injury • Report a problem • Talk about preventing workplace injuries • Talk about workplace health and safety • Give an opinion	• Read closely • Respond to text-dependent questions • Cite evidence • Build vocabulary • Write about workplace health and safety	• Read about preventing workplace stress injuries • Fill out an employee injury report	• Follow directions: learn to safely lift and move a box • Solve problems • Paraphrasing

4   Scope and Sequence

Unit, Title, Pages	Theme	Career Clusters and Occupations	Language Functions	College and Career Readiness Skills	Informational Text	Critical Thinking, Problem Solving, and Paraphrasing
Unit 4 **A Schedule Conflict** Pages 32–37	• Reading a work schedule • Employees trading shifts • Communication between employer and employee	Transportation: auto repair • Automotive service technicians • Supervisor Manufacturing: furniture factory • Factory worker	• Talk about work schedules • Discuss a punctuality problem • Give advice about a schedule conflict • Talk about reasons for being late or missing work • Talk about work skills	• Read closely • Respond to text-dependent questions • Cite evidence • Retell a story • Build vocabulary • Write about soft skills • Internet Research: work skills	• Read about workplace soft skills • Read a work schedule	• Critical thinking: categorize • Solve problems • Self-inventory: soft skills
Unit 5 **A Dangerous Decision** Pages 38–43	• Workplace safety: safety equipment • Preventing workplace injury	Construction: small business • Handyman Manufacturing: airplane factory • Factory worker	• Talk about wearing safety equipment • Discuss a workplace injury • Describe a medical problem • Give an opinion	• Read closely • Respond to text-dependent questions • Cite evidence • Retell a story • Build vocabulary • Write about workplace health and safety	• Read about OSHA rules	• Critical thinking: draw conclusions • Solve problems
Unit 6 **A Computer Lesson** Pages 44–49	• Basic computer skills • Adult education and continuing education classes	Education: information technology instruction • Computer teacher	• Talk about using computers • Discuss doing internet research • Discuss following instructions • Give instructions for the ergonomic use of a computer • Compare computer skills and classroom and workplace skills	• Read closely • Respond to text-dependent questions • Cite evidence • Build vocabulary • Learn how to use internet search skills • Write about using computer skills at work and at school • Internet Research: free basic computer skills training	• Read instructions to create, save, and print a document	• Critical thinking: draw conclusions • Critical thinking: categorizing

Unit, Title, Pages	Theme	Career Clusters and Occupations	Language Functions	College and Career Readiness Skills	Informational Text	Critical Thinking, Problem Solving, and Paraphrasing
Unit 7 **Be Productive!** Pages 50–55	• Reading a work order • Being evaluated on the job • Warnings and write-ups	Sales: discount store • Stock clerks • Team leader	• Talk about reading and following directions on a work order • Talk about productivity • Interpret a work order • Discuss teamwork skills • Give an opinion	• Read closely • Respond to text-dependent questions • Cite evidence • Build vocabulary • Review a story • Write about productive work habits	• Read about technology and teamwork	• Critical thinking: matching • Self-inventory: teamwork skills • Critical thinking: categorizing
Unit 8 **Paycheck Problem** Pages 56–61	• Paychecks and pay stubs • Requesting a payroll adjustment • Communication between employer and employee	Government: mail delivery • Mail carrier • Postal supervisor Construction: janitor	• Talk about paychecks, paystubs, and payroll errors • Discuss negotiating with a landlord to pay rent late • Discuss deductions • Discuss jobs paying more than the minimum wage	• Read closely • Respond to text-dependent questions • Cite evidence • Build vocabulary • Retell a story • Internet Research: minimum wage • Write about the minimum wage and jobs paying above minimum wage	• Read a pay stub	• Solve problems • Critical thinking: matching
Unit 9 **A Safety Meeting** Pages 62–67	• Workplace safety • Safe use of heavy equipment: forklift • Safety meetings	Distribution: warehousing and shipping • Shipping clerk • Assistant shipping clerk	• Talk about following safety rules • Discuss workplace safety • Talk about taking notes in a safety meeting	• Read closely • Respond to text-dependent questions • Cite evidence • Build vocabulary • Summarize information • Write about a safe workplace • Internet Research: OSHA workplace safety rules	• Read a list of safety rules	• Paraphrasing • Critical thinking: draw conclusions • Solve problems

Unit, Title, Pages	Theme	Career Clusters and Occupations	Language Functions	College and Career Readiness Skills	Informational Text	Critical Thinking, Problem Solving, and Paraphrasing
Unit 10 **A Dose of Medicine** Pages 68–73	• Health care • Providing medication • Soft skills: customer service skills • Hard skills: technical skills	Health sciences: pharmacy • Pharmacy technician • Pharmacist	• Talk about reading a medicine label on a prescription bottle • Discuss dosages of medication and when to take medication • Talk about getting a flu shot • Talk about the job skills of a pharmacy technician and a pharmacist • Give an opinion	• Read closely • Respond to text-dependent questions • Cite evidence • Build vocabulary • Retell a story • Review a story • Write about getting a job as a pharmacy technician or a pharmacist	• Read about getting a flu shot	• Critical thinking: categorizing
Unit 11 **Get Promoted** Pages 74–79	• Technology • Getting a promotion and a pay raise • On-the-job training • Having a performance evaluation	Manufacturing: safety equipment production • Maintenance mechanic • Sewing machine operator • Supervisor	• Talk about getting a promotion • Talk about a performance evaluation • Discuss on-the-job training • Discuss technology in the workplace • Compare old and new machinery	• Read closely • Respond to text-dependent questions • Cite evidence • Build vocabulary • Summarize information • Review a story • Write about your technology skills	• Read about using technology in the workplace	• Self-inventory: technology skills • Solve problems
Unit 12 **Returning to Normal** Pages 80–85	• Health care • Physical therapy • Natural healing	Health sciences: therapeutic services • Physical therapist • Physical therapy aide	• Talk about work responsibilities • Discuss working under supervision • Discuss educational and career plans • Describe physical problems to a doctor • Give an opinion	• Read closely • Respond to text-dependent questions • Cite evidence • Build vocabulary • Write about future jobs in physical and occupational therapy • Internet Research: jobs in physical and occupational therapy	• Read about what physical therapists do on the job	• Critical thinking: matching • Solve problems

TO THE TEACHER

Increasingly, the U.S. labor market demands a higher level of preparedness from its labor force. Where basic work and communication skills were once sufficient, employers now expect workers to be proficient in the areas of interpersonal communication, cooperation and problem-solving, job-specific hard skills, and technology. In addition, employers seek out candidates with higher levels of academic knowledge and skills (college and career readiness skills) in the areas of academic language, reading, writing, and critical thinking.

Adult English language learners (ELLs) often feel challenged as they make their way into the workforce and attempt to move up to higher positions. Mastering language and college and career readiness skills will allow adult ELLs to create and maintain a higher quality of life for themselves and their families. The *Road to Work* series provides scaffolded support for high-beginning and intermediate level ELLs as they acquire the language, employability skills, and content knowledge needed to obtain jobs and become successful employees.

Road to Work meaningfully engages ELLs in all aspects of the job hunting and job attainment process: from career research and job search to job investigation and job application, from job interviewing and job attainment to on-the-job navigation and problem-solving. In *Choosing a Job Path*, the first book in the series, students assess and build their own skills while exploring career options. In *Applying and Interviewing*, the second book in the series, students learn about the job application and interview process. In *Succeeding on the Job*, the third book, students meet real workers and collaborate on resolutions to everyday workplace issues.

Road to Work recognizes the importance of building the necessary college and career readiness and English language proficiency skills, such as oral communication, reading complex informational text, using academic vocabulary, online researching, and the application of critical thinking, and collaboration. *Road to Work* guides students in skill development as they learn to cite evidence, build academic vocabulary and language, and build content and background knowledge. ELLs develop these skills on the pages of the *Road to Work* series through a variety of interactive activities that provide the language, skill, and technological onramps students need to continue moving successfully along academic and career pathways.

Through close reading and collaborative discussion of the high-interest stories and informational articles in *Road to Work*, students become actively engaged in situations involving customer service, workplace safety, teamwork and responsibility, following instructions and thinking independently, soft skill development, light and heavy equipment use, computer and internet skills, workplace habits and responsibilities, workplace promotion and discipline, and education and training. While building close reading skills, students learn to construct meaning from complex text, use academic language and workplace vocabulary, and cite evidence in support of claims. They develop critical thinking and problem-solving skills. Students using the text are guided to work both individually and collaboratively, in pairs or teams, and along with the whole class.

Road to Work recognizes the significance of teaching the soft skills, hard skills, and computer skills that will help students succeed on a job. Soft skills such as getting along with others, having a positive attitude, dependability, responsibility, punctuality, and teamwork are stressed throughout the text. The hard skills required on specific jobs are identified in several units.

The academic, language, and employability skills students develop while engaged with the text are transferable from the classroom to the workplace. A student who develops the soft skill of working in a team while practicing with *Road to Work* will transfer that skill to the workplace. Students who develop critical thinking and problem solving skills in the classroom will be able to use those same skills on the job. Students who develop close reading and critical thinking skills will apply those skills as they read a workplace memo or safety report. Students, having discussed workplace safety in the classroom, will bring a deeper understanding of the issue to their jobs.

Texts in the *Road to Work* series may be used as core readers or as supplements in English as a Second Language (ESL), Vocational ESL (VESL), or Career and Technical Education (CTE) classes. Or, they may be used within other vocational programs such as Integrated Educational Training (IET), Integrated Basic Skills and Educational Training (IBEST). The stories in the books are non-sequential, providing the flexibility to be taught in any order.

Using Road to Work: Succeeding on the Job

The readings in *Succeeding on the Job* help students assess and build their own college and career readiness skills while exploring the themes of providing quality patient care, maintaining occupational health and safety, providing good customer service, working on a team, communication between employers and employees, preventing on-the-job injuries, using technology in the workplace, soft and hard workplace skills, and training on the job. Students learn by closely reading a pay stub, a work schedule, safety rules, and a patient's chart. They learn to create documents and fill out an Employee Injury Report. Stories and informational readings in *Succeeding on the Job* encompass a variety of industrial sectors including manufacturing, construction, health sciences, hospitality, retail sales, transportation, educational services, government, and distribution.

Unit Preview

Introduce students to a unit through class discussion of the opening picture, story title, and pre-reading questions. Ask pre-reading questions to create interest in the unit theme and to provide a starting point for discussion.

Begin the unit with a whole class pre-reading discussion to activate students' background knowledge and known vocabulary, and to contextualize new content-based academic vocabulary. Ask pre-reading questions to guide students to context clues in the picture and title. *Look at the picture. What is the chef doing? Why does he put salt in the food?*

- Prior to reading, introduce the story. *Today we're going to read a story about a man who fixes things inside and outside a house. Look at the picture. Do you know the name of his job? That's right. He's a handyman.*

- Ask additional pre-reading questions. *Who do you see in the picture? Where is she/he? What is she/he doing? What's her/his job? What does she/he do on the job? What do you think this story is about? What do you think is going to happen?*

- New vocabulary words are bolded in the reading. Definitions for these words are in the glossary at the back of the book.

- Introduce new vocabulary by asking story-related questions. *Why do you think the pharmacy tech is counting pills in a tray? Why do you think the cook is wearing an oven mitt on his hand? Why do you think the Certified Nursing Assistant is taking the patient's blood pressure?* As new vocabulary words are introduced, explain the words, and list them on the board.

- Pre-teach any critical vocabulary words. *In this unit, the workers go to a mandatory safety meeting. "Mandatory" means the workers have to go to the meeting. "Mandatory" means no one can be absent from the meeting. Did you ever have to go to a mandatory meeting?* Write the critical vocabulary words on the board.

  Note: For additional suggestions on how to teach vocabulary, see Vocabulary Exercises on page 11.

- **Extensions:**

  » After modeling the questions and answers with the whole class, have student pairs or groups ask and discuss the pre-reading questions.

  » Have student groups generate additional questions about the title and opening picture and share their questions with the class.

Opening Story

Unit opener stories in the text introduce realistic characters. All the characters and problems they encounter in *Succeeding on the Job* are based on real-life situations. Each story introduces the unit theme while contextualizing new vocabulary in a workplace setting.

Close Reading: First Read The first time students encounter a story in the text, ask them to read for general understanding (gist).

- See information on pre-teaching critical vocabulary under Unit Preview (page 9) and Vocabulary Exercises (page 11). Ask pre-reading questions that guide students to understand new vocabulary words. *In today's story, a physical therapy aide helps an injured patient. Were you, or someone you know ever in an accident? Were you hurt or injured? Did you need physical therapy after the accident?* Have students listen and silently read along as the teacher reads the story aloud to the class. Stop after each sentence or paragraph to discuss new vocabulary words and clarify meanings.

- Call on students to re-read sentences or a paragraph of the story aloud to the class.

- Develop focused listening skills by telling students what to listen for before paragraphs are introduced. *Class, today we are going to talk about a woman in medicine. Listen for the name of her job. Listen for how many hours she works every day. Listen for why she decides to become a Certified Nursing Assistant.*

- Discuss and contextualize unfamiliar vocabulary words while presenting the story. See Vocabulary Exercises on page 11.

- After reading a paragraph, ask predictive questions about the next paragraph: *What protective clothing do you think the handyman puts on before he starts working? What do you think the employees learned at the safety meeting?*

Close Reading: Additional Readings Close reading is the careful re-reading of complex text. When asked the right questions during close reading, students read more deeply in the search for meaning. They search for main idea and detail. They use critical thinking to summarize and infer, to compare and contrast information.

- **Check Your Understanding** follows the opening story in each unit of *Succeeding on the Job*. Text dependent questions (TDQs) guide students to read more deeply, find and cite evidence, search for detail, summarize information, and make inferences.

  » In responding to TDQs, students are guided to use academic phrases such as *According to the story…*, or, *In paragraph 2 of the story…* when citing evidence. Citing evidence is a transferable skill. The ability to cite evidence has been found to enhance student credibility and respectability in the real world.

- **Story Retell** challenges student pairs to review both the main idea and details of the story as they discuss the sequence of events. During the *Chronological Picture Story Retell*, students practice key vocabulary words and phrases while working with content-related pictures and summarizing statements. Encourage students to use sequencing words (*first, second, third; first, next, then*) while retelling the story. *First Mr. Millman looks at the menu and orders garlic shrimp. Next Eddie Chan cooks garlic shrimp in the restaurant kitchen. Then ….*

- When the reading is complete, review the answers to questions asked during the close reading activities. *So, why did she decide to become a Certified Nursing Assistant?* Help students summarize the general themes of the story. *What was the story about? In this story we learned about a cook who prepared food that a customer did not like.*

- **Extension:** Have students re-read the story together in pairs or groups. Each student reads a paragraph. Students review story content and vocabulary while answering the text dependent questions. They summarize the story. *This story is about a worker who came to work late. His boss was angry.*

Vocabulary Exercises

Expanding academic language, vocabulary, and content knowledge is key to enabling students to function and succeed both academically and in the workforce. In *Succeeding on the Job*, new vocabulary words are introduced in the context of the opening stories and informational readings. From 14 to 20 vocabulary terms are introduced in each unit. A glossary is included at the back of the book.

Vocabulary Building exercises help students expand their understanding of and practice with new words.

- Pre-teach any critical vocabulary words. (See information in the Unit Preview and Close Reading sections.)

- Discuss and contextualize new vocabulary words while teaching the story. *Class, in paragraph 6, please underline the word "collaborate." In today's story, Pierre, a computer teacher, teaches his students to collaborate. They work together in groups. Why do you think it's important to collaborate at school? At work?* List all the new vocabulary words on the board.

- Have students pay attention to new vocabulary words as they read the story. Guide students to annotate (circle, underline, or highlight) new vocabulary words.

- Move around the class discussing, repeating, and reinforcing new vocabulary words and phrases. *The handyman removed the window. He replaced it with another.*

- Have students complete the vocabulary practice on their own and review the vocabulary words and meanings with a partner.

- Build in additional vocabulary practice using pictures and flash cards of workplace locations, occupations, interactions on the job, workplace safety issues, etc.

- Create weekly vocabulary tests to help students learn the new vocabulary words.

- Refer students to the definitions of words in the glossary at the back of the book.

- Have students create a notebook dictionary or vocabulary database in their computer in which they list each new vocabulary word, its definition, and a sentence containing the word.

- **Extensions:**

  » Have students create their own flash cards and review word meanings with partners.

  » Form teams of four. Have each student choose two new words from the unit and write each word on a separate piece of paper. Put the words in a pile. Have one person in the group draw a word. The student pronounces the word and gives a definition. Then the student makes a sentence with the word, or reads a sentence from the story containing the word. Team members provide help as needed.

Talk About Work: Dialog

Each unit in *Succeeding on the Job* contains a dialog related to the employee from the opening story. During each dialog a problem is presented. The partner in the dialog, perhaps a co-worker, supervisor, friend, teacher, or counselor, offers meaningful advice. These dialogs model typical career-building and workplace-related conversations. They provide students with useful language for discussing work-related issues.

- Set the scene for the dialog. *You are the chef in a restaurant. The manager is talking to you about a problem with a customer. Two shipping clerks just attended a safety meeting. They are reviewing how to safely drive a forklift.*

- Have student pairs practice the dialog. After, have pairs practice the dialog with other pairs, or in front of the class.

Read About Work: Informational Reading

At work, students will be expected to read and comprehend emails, memos, safety manuals, work orders, and a variety of print or online texts. The short informational readings in *Succeeding on the Job* highlight both the content knowledge and knowledge of forms students need to function effectively in the workplace. From tips for good customer service to reading about ways to prevent workplace stress injuries, from tips on creating a document to reading the details of a patient's medical chart, these informational readings build the background knowledge students need to succeed in the workplace.

- **Text-Dependent Comprehension Questions (TDQs)** guide students to read more deeply, search for essential details, summarize information, find and cite evidence, and make inferences from the content. Teachers can guide students to respond to the TDQs by using phrases such as, "According to Rita's schedule,…" or "According to the safety rules, …".

- **Workplace Documents** in *Succeeding on the Job* provide students the opportunity to learn to read and interpret safety rules, look carefully at work schedules and pay stubs, and to fill out an injury report form. All of these documents are typical of today's workplace.

  » Encourage students to bring authentic workplace documents from their jobs, or the jobs of others, such as work schedules, safety manuals, injury report forms, etc. Discuss the purpose of these workplace documents with the class. Keep a class notebook of these documents which can be referenced.

- **Team Talk** provides student working in teams the opportunity to collaboratively discuss their points of view on important work-related issues such as having a safe and healthy workplace, punctuality, using technology skills on the job, providing quality patient care, preventing workplace injuries, and providing quality customer service.

Self-Assessment, Self-Evaluation, Self-Inventory

In connection with the informational readings, students are asked to evaluate their own soft and hard workplace skills and abilities to perform workplace tasks. As an employer on the job would evaluate a worker, students are asked to self-evaluate. They learn to make statements about their strengths: *I can cooperate with others. I can work in a team.* They consider areas where they are strong and areas where their skills need improvement.

Role Play

Drama and role play bring characters to life. During the role play activity, student pairs enact scenes that would normally take place in real time. While using guided language, students learn to communicate appropriately with fellow workers, patients, fellow students and customers. Teachers may want to use role play situations as a way of assessing a student's ability to integrate and activate content material.

Critical Thinking: Problem Solving

Problem solving tasks engage student teams in discussing the kinds of workplace situations they may expect to confront at work. Given a list of options, students talk together about the pros and cons of handling on-the-job issues. Observing the way students work in problem-solving groups can help teachers assess student mastery of vocabulary and unit content.

- Have students form groups of four. Ask each group to select a leader, a recorder, a reporter, and a timekeeper.

- Have the group leader read the problem. The timekeeper allots one to two minutes for each team member to give their opinion about the best option. Next, the group discusses the pros and cons of each solution and comes to an agreement about the best solution. The recorder will take notes. The reporter shares the group's decision with the class. *Our group thinks that she/he can ….*

Critical Thinking: Matching, Categorizing, Paraphrasing

Critical thinking skills activities prepare students for the kinds of evaluative tasks they may be asked to do on the job. Determining which work habits are good and which are bad, determining appropriate reasons for being late or missing work, and summarizing computer and workplace skills all build muscle for on-the-job decision making.

In Other Words

This activity extends both the academic vocabulary practice and critical thinking skills developed within the unit. Students stretch their use of language by substituting new vocabulary words in sentences.

Summarizing, paraphrasing, and rephrasing of information are important skills for those entering the workforce. At work, in a variety of situations, an employee may be asked to summarize the boss's instructions. *What did the boss say?* In Other Words exercises provide students preliminary practice with building these important skills.

- **Extension:**

  » To reinforce lesson vocabulary, student pairs and groups play *What's Another Word for …?* They start with a known word, and substitute the lesson vocabulary word.

  A. *What's another word for* stop*?*
  B. Prevent.
  A. *Make a sentence with the word.*
  B. *A safety harness prevents a worker from falling.*
  A. *Excellent!*

Review the Story

Near the end of a unit, Review the Story encourages student pairs to fill in and review vocabulary and content information from the reading while summarizing what happened.

- After students practice the review, guide students back to the story. Ask summarizing questions: *What is this story about? What did you learn from this story?*

Talk and Write

Talk and Write invites students to work first in teams, and then individually, to build on the content information they've read and discussed in the unit. Students summarize their own experiences, give opinions based on the information read and their experiences, and make inferences. They share their writing with other team members.

- **Extension:** After students complete the writing and sharing activity, have them count off from one to four. Have students one and two move to a different group and share and discuss their answers with the new team.

Internet Research

These extension activities direct students to use an internet search engine to find out information or to answer a question. These activities offer important practice for the workplace as well as addressing computer and internet research skills that are integral to standards such as the College and Career Readiness Standards and the English Language Proficiency Standards for writing.

UNIT 1

Providing Patient Care

▶ *Look at the picture. What is the woman doing?*

▶ *Read the title. What do you think the story is about?*

1   Joy works the **day shift** in a hospital. She is a Certified Nursing Assistant (CNA). She helps **patients** with the **activities of daily living**. Joy helps patients get out of bed, go to the bathroom, brush their teeth, take a shower, get dressed, and eat.

2   Joy takes each patient's **temperature** and **blood pressure**. She asks patients how they are feeling. She asks, "Are you dizzy?" and, "Where does it hurt?" Joy helps patients walk.

3   How did Joy learn to be a CNA? First she took a Personal Care Assistant class for English language learners. Joy learned the English vocabulary and medical skills needed to be a **caregiver**. She learned about hand washing. She learned about lifting and turning a **bedridden** patient. She learned about moving a patient to a **wheelchair**.

4   Joy also learned to make **small talk**. She says, "You look nice today." She asks, "Did you watch TV this morning?"

5   Next Joy took a CNA class where she learned more skills. She learned to take **vital signs** (blood pressure and temperature). She learned **anatomy**. She got **on-the-job experience** at a nursing home.

6   At the end of the CNA class, Joy took two tests. She passed a written test with 100 questions. After that, she took a patient care test to show that she could do the work. After Joy passed both tests, she **received** a **certificate** from her state. Now she is a state-certified CNA.

Check Your Understanding

Answer the questions. Talk with a partner.

1.   What shift does Joy work in the hospital? _____

2.   What is Joy's occupation? _____

3.   Look at paragraph 1. What are two examples of activities of daily living?
_____

4.   Look at paragraph 3. What are three skills Joy learned in the Personal Care Assistant class? _____

5.   Give an example of small talk. _____

6.   According to paragraph 5, what are vital signs? _____

7.   Joy studied the human body in her CNA class. She learned _____

8.   Which two tests did Joy take? _____

9.   In paragraph _____, Joy received a CNA certificate from her state.

10. Why do you think Joy asks patients, "Are you dizzy?" _____

Vocabulary Building

Circle the word or phrase that means the same as the vocabulary word(s). Talk about your answers with a partner.

1. Joy works the *day shift* in a hospital.

    a. work time in the day

    b. work time at night

2. She takes each patient's *temperature*.

    a. measure of how fast the heart is beating

    b. measure of how warm the body is

3. She learned about lifting and turning a *bedridden patient*.

    a. person who can't get out of bed

    b. person who can walk

4. Joy learned to make *small talk*.

    a. conversation about important decisions

    b. conversation about easy things to talk about

5. In her CNA class, Joy learned *anatomy*.

    a. the human body

    b. animals

In Other Words

Work with a partner. Choose the words that mean the same. Fill in the correct words. Read the new sentences.

1. Joy and Elizabeth work the day shift.

    _____ go to work _____.

You, They .... in the morning, at night

2. Joy got on-the-job experience in a nursing home.

    _____ got _____ in a nursing home.

She, He .... work practice, test practice

3. Joy helps patients and takes their temperature and blood pressure.

    Joy helps _____ and takes their _____.

sick people, caregivers .... anatomy, vital signs

Talk About Work: Taking Career Education Classes

Practice the dialog with a partner.

Elizabeth: I'm not sure what career I want. I like working with people, and I like nursing.

Afra: Why don't you try the two classes I took: Personal Care Assistant and Certified Nursing Assistant?

Elizabeth: Do you think my English is OK?

Afra: Your English is fine. I learned a lot in those health careers classes! The teachers were wonderful. They taught us the English vocabulary for health care. They taught us to work with patients.

Elizabeth: When do classes begin?

Afra: In September. All the information is online. Look at the school's website.

Elizabeth: OK. I'll look at the website. Would you come with me when I **register**?

Afra: Sure. I'd be glad to.

Team Talk
Talk with your teammates.

- What did Afra learn in her classes?

- What should Elizabeth do?

- What classes would you like to take?

- Why is providing patient care an important and difficult job?

Read About Work: A Patient Chart

Read the patient chart with a partner. Answer the questions.

Yvette is in the hospital. A CNA checks her vital signs every morning. They are recorded on a chart. The chart also shows what **normal**, or healthy, vital signs are. The doctor reviews the chart.

PATIENT CHART

Patient's Name Yvette Parker		Date of Birth July 30, 1990
Physician's Name Dr. David Suttles		
Vital Signs:	**Normal**	**Patient**
Blood Pressure	120/80	140/90
Body Temperature	97.6–99.6 F	98.1
Breathing Rate	12–20 breaths per minute	30

1. What is the patient's date of birth? _____

2. Who is the patient's doctor? _____

3. What is a normal blood pressure? _____

4. What is the patient's blood pressure? _____

5. Is the patient's blood pressure normal? _____

Critical Thinking: Problem Solving

Read the problem. Check the good ideas. Write another good idea on the line. Discuss your ideas with your teammates.

Masud works with patients in a rehabilitation center. He walks the patients around the floor. Masud helps turn patients in their beds. He helps move patients from the bed to a wheelchair. Every day Masud's back hurts from moving and lifting patients. What can he do?

☐ Masud can take aspirin for the pain.

☐ Masud can ask for an assistant to help him lift patients.

☐ Masud can ask his employer to pay for him to see a doctor.

☐ Masud can go back to school and study for another job.

☐ Masud can _____

Role Play: In a Skilled Nursing Center
Practice the dialog with a partner.

Student A: You are a Personal Care Assistant at a skilled nursing center. You need to move a patient to a wheelchair. You tell the patient what you are doing. You say:

- Good morning, _____.

- How are you feeling today?

- I'm going to move you into your wheelchair.

- Are you ready?

- First I'm going to move you to the edge of the bed.

- Can you put your legs over the side?

- I'm going to lift you now.

- Don't worry; I won't let you fall.

- Are you comfortable?

Student B: You are the patient. You are in bed. You want to be sitting in a wheelchair. The caregiver is moving you. You respond to the caregiver.

Talk and Write
Talk with a partner. Write about your English skills. Write about a job you are looking for.

What is your level of English? _____

What job are you (or is someone you know) looking for? _____

_____

What level of English do you need for that job? _____

What education and training do you need for that job? _____

_____

UNIT 2

The Customer Is Always Right

▶ *Look at the picture. What is the chef doing?*

▶ *Why does he put salt in the food?*

1   Eddie Chan is a **chef**. He works in a Chinese **restaurant**. Every day Eddie stands in front of a hot stove. He **prepares** food in a **wok**. He wears an **apron** to **protect** his body and an **oven mitt** to protect his hand.

2   Today Eddie is cooking garlic shrimp for Mr. Millman, a **regular customer**. Mr. Millman always orders shrimp.

3   When the wok is hot, Eddie cooks the shrimp with vegetables. He adds extra salt to give the shrimp a good **flavor**. The shrimp smells wonderful.

4   The server brings the garlic shrimp to the customer. She puts the plate on the table. She says, "Here's your garlic shrimp. Enjoy!"

5   Mr. Millman looks at the shrimp and smiles. He takes a bite. He **chokes**. He coughs. He drinks some water. Then he drinks more water.

6   "This shrimp is too salty," he tells the **server**. "I can't eat it. Take it back."

7   The server talks to the restaurant **manager**. She says, "Mr. Millman is not happy. He wants a new order of shrimp."

8   The restaurant manager **apologizes**. The manager says, "I am so sorry. We'll make you some shrimp with no salt. Our restaurant rule is: **The customer is always right!**"

Check Your Understanding

Answer the questions. Talk with a partner.

1.   What is Eddie Chan's job? _____

2.   According to paragraph 1, where does he work? _____

3.   What does Eddie Chan do on his job? _____

4.   Look at paragraph 1. What is another word for *pan* in the story? _____

5.   What **protective clothing** does Eddie wear on the job? _____

6.   According to paragraph 2, what does the customer order? _____

7.   According to paragraph 6, why is Mr. Millman unhappy with his food? _____

_____

8.   What is the restaurant's rule? _____

9.   In paragraph _____, the manager apologizes. He tells the customer, "I am so sorry."

10. In paragraph _____, the customer chokes on his shrimp. He drinks some water.

Story Retell

Number the pictures and sentences in the correct order. Retell the story.

a. _____
Mr. Millman complains to the server.

b. _____
Mr. Millman looks at the menu and orders garlic shrimp.

c. _____
The customer eats the salty shrimp.

d. _____
The restaurant manager tells Mr. Millman, "I am so sorry. The customer is always right!"

e. _____
Eddie Chan cooks garlic shrimp in the restaurant kitchen.

Vocabulary Building

Circle the word or phrase that means the same as the vocabulary word(s). Talk about your answers with a partner.

1. Eddie Chan is a *chef*.

    a. cook   b. manager

2. The restaurant manager *apologizes* to Mr. Millman.

    a. says he isn't interested   b. says he's sorry

3. Mr. Millman *is a regular customer*.

    a. comes to the restaurant for the first time   b. comes to the restaurant often

4. Mr. Millman *chokes on his food*.

    a. gets food stuck in his throat   b. eats all the hot food

5. The *server* talks to the restaurant manager.

    a. person who brings your food   b. chef

 **Talk About Work: A Customer Complaint**

Practice the dialog with a partner.

Manager: Eddie, we have a problem. The customer says his shrimp is too salty.

Eddie: I'm sorry. I put in extra salt. I wanted the shrimp to have good flavor.

Manager: Shrimp is already salty. It comes from the ocean. Ocean water is salty. Don't add extra salt.

Eddie: Thank you for telling me. I won't do that again.

Manager: Eddie, please make a new order. Remember our rule: The customer is always right!

Critical Thinking: What Did Eddie Learn?

Circle the correct answers. Talk about your answers with a partner.

1. a. You need to listen to the boss.

   b. You don't need to listen to the boss.

2. a. You don't need to follow instructions.

   b. You need to follow instructions.

3. a. The customer is always right.

   b. The customer is never right.

4. a. Shrimp isn't salty.

   b. Shrimp is salty.

In Other Words

Work with a partner. Choose the words that mean the same. Fill in the correct words. Read the new sentences.

1. Every day Eddie <u>prepares</u> food in a <u>wok</u>.

   Every day he _____ food in a _____.
                         eats, cooks   pan, bowl

2. The server says, "<u>Mr. Millman</u> is not happy with his <u>order</u>."

   The server says, "_____ is not happy with his _____."
                          the customer, the owner   food, bill

Read About Work: Good Customer Service

Read these tips for restaurant servers.

Seven Tips for Good Customer Service

- ☑ Be friendly and smile. Say hello to new customers.
- ☑ Seat customers at a table quickly. Give them a menu.
- ☑ Don't make customers wait. Five to ten minutes after you give customers a menu, take their order.
- ☑ Listen carefully. Write down what customers want.
- ☑ Bring the food when it is hot. No one likes cold food.
- ☑ Make customers feel comfortable. Ask, "Is there anything else I can get for you?"
- ☑ Thank customers. Say, "Thank you for coming. We hope to see you again soon."

Team Talk

Review the tips. Talk with your teammates about good customer service. What are three things restaurant servers say to their customers?

Role Play: Using Customer Service Language
Practice the dialog with a partner.

Student A: You are a customer. It is lunchtime. You are hungry. You go to a restaurant. The restaurant is busy. You want to eat lunch quickly and go back to work.

Student B: You are a server in the restaurant. You are busy. You find a table for the customer. Use good customer service language:

- May I help you?

- I'm sorry you had to wait.

- Can I get you something to drink?

- Are you ready to order?

- I'm sorry, that was my mistake. Let me bring you another _____.

- Would you like some dessert?

- Thank you for coming. I hope to see you soon.

Talk and Write
Talk with a partner about customer service. Write about good and bad customer service.

What is good customer service? _____

_____

Why is good customer service at a restaurant important? _____

_____

_____

Did you ever experience bad customer service? What happened? _____

_____

_____

Be Healthy and Safe at Work

▶ *Look at the picture. Where is the cashier? What is she doing?*

▶ *Read the title. What do you think "work safe" means?*

1   Maria Gonzalez works at Fresh Foods Market. She's a **full-time cashier**. Maria has worked at the same **supermarket** for ten years. Her husband, Julio, works in construction.

2   Maria uses a **scanner** at work every day. Maria picks up items and moves them across the scanner window. The scanner **scans**, or reads, the **bar code** on each item. The machine scans the bar codes on soup and cereal. The machine scans and weighs vegetables and fruits.

3   Sometimes Maria turns the **packages** to find the bar code. She **twists** her **wrist** to scan the code. When an item doesn't scan, Maria enters the bar code number on the computer keyboard.

4   Maria's been doing the same **repetitive motion** at work for ten years. Every day she moves items across the scanner. Her hands and wrists **hurt**. The pain makes it hard for Maria to smile at customers.

5   "I don't know what to do," Maria tells Julio. "If I **complain**, I can **lose my job**!"

6   "Talk to your boss," Julio says. "Tell him about the problem. For now, put some ice on it. But maybe you need to see a doctor."

7   "OK," says Maria. "That's a good idea. I'll talk to my boss tomorrow."

Check Your Understanding

Answer the questions. Talk with a partner.

1. What is Maria's job? _____

2. According to the story, does Maria work full time or part time? _____

3. In paragraph 2, what machine does Maria use on her job? _____

4. What does the scanner do? _____

5. According to paragraph 2, what does Maria do on her job? _____

   _____

6. In paragraph 3, why does Maria need to twist her wrist? _____

7. In which paragraph do you find the words *repetitive motion*? _____

8. Look back at the story. Why do Maria's hands and wrists hurt? _____

   _____

9. Paragraph _____ tells what the scanner does.

10. In paragraph _____, Julio tells Maria to talk to her boss about the problem.

Vocabulary Building

Circle the sentence that means the same. Talk about your answers with a partner.

1. Maria Gonzalez works at Fresh Foods Market. *She's a cashier.*

   a. Maria sweeps the supermarket floor.
   b. Maria scans food items. She takes cash, checks, and credit cards.

2. The machine *scans* the bar codes on soup and cereal.

   a. It reads the information on packages.
   b. It turns on and off.

3. Maria's hands and wrists *hurt.*

   a. She feels pain.
   b. She feels no pain.

4. Moving her hands across the scanner every day is a *repetitive motion*.

   a. She doesn't use her hands at work.
   b. She moves her hands the same way at work many times every day.

5. Maria says *"If I complain, I can lose my job!"*

   a. She wants to talk about her problem.
   b. She doesn't want to tell her boss about her problem.

Talk About Work: Reporting a Health Problem at Work

Practice the dialog with a partner.

Mr. Washington: How can I help you, Maria?

Maria: I have a problem. When I use the scanner at work, my hands and wrists hurt.

Mr. Washington: Does this happen every day, or only sometimes, Maria?

Maria: It happens every time I use the scanner.

Mr. Washington: Did you take your break today, Maria? Did you rest your hands?

Maria: Yes. I always rest my hands when I take a break.

Mr. Washington: I'll look into your problem, Maria. You need to fill out an **Injury Report** form. Take a look at your **safety manual**. Review the chapter on scanning.

Fill Out a Form: Maria's Employee Injury Report

Pairs. Talk with your partner. Fill out the form for Maria.

Employee Injury Report

Employee name: _____   Job title: _____

Date and time of injury: _____

Describe the injury:

_____

_____

Describe what happened and where:

_____

_____

In Other Words

Work with a partner. Choose the words that mean the same. Fill in the correct words. Read the new sentences.

1. Maria works at a <u>supermarket</u>. She uses a <u>scanner</u> every day.

   Maria works at a _____. *She uses a* _____ *every day.*
                   large market, small market   sewing machine, machine that reads bar codes

2. Maria <u>twists</u> the <u>packages</u> to find the bar code.

   Maria _____ *the* _____ *to find the bar code.*
                opens, turns   containers, vegetables

3. The pain in <u>Maria's</u> wrists can <u>get worse</u>.

   The pain in _____ *wrists can* _____ *.*
               his, her   increase, decrease

Workplace Activity: Safely Moving a Box

First practice the activity with your teacher. Next practice with a partner. One student reads the directions. One student follows the directions. Then change places.

1. You are at work. You are going to move a heavy box.

2. Bend your knees and **squat down**.

3. Pull in your stomach muscles.

4. Keep your back straight.

5. Put your hands around the box.

6. Slowly pick up the box.

7. Hold the box close to your body. (Hug the box.)

8. Stand up and walk across the room with the box.

9. Bend your knees and slowly put down the box.

10. Smile. Your work is complete!

Role Play: A Workplace Safety Problem

Practice the dialog with a partner.

Student A: You are Mario, a stock clerk at Fresh Foods Market. You lift boxes of cans off the floor and put them on a cart.

You know the safe way to lift a box is to squat down. Your boss, Mr. Washington, showed you how to squat down and lift a box correctly. Sometimes you forget and bend from the waist to pick up a box.

Student B: You are Mr. Washington, Mario's boss. Yesterday, you saw Mario bend over to pick up some boxes. Today, you talk to Mario. You tell Mario to be more careful.

Read About Work: Avoiding Workplace Stress Injuries

Read this information about workplace injuries.

Doing the same motion over and over again, day after day, can cause pain. This is called **repetitive stress injury (RSI)**. The pain can be in your fingers, hands, neck, or back. You can get RSI working at a computer, at a supermarket checkout counter, or on an assembly line. Bad posture, sitting at a computer for many hours a day, or working under stress can cause RSI.

What can you do to avoid RSI?

- At a desk:
    » Sit up straight in your chair. Support your back.
    » Place your computer screen at eye level.
    » Rest your feet on the floor.
    » Take regular breaks.
    » Stand up and **stretch**. Get up and move around every hour.
- To pick something up: Don't bend from the waist. Squat down.
- To relax: **Take deep breaths.**

Team Talk

Review the information. Talk with your teammates. There are some things you can do to keep from getting RSI. According to the article, what are three things you can do to avoid RSI?

Talk and Write

Talk with a partner about workplace health and safety. Then write about your job or a job you want.

Are you doing any repetitive motion on your job? Explain. _____

_____

Are there other health or safety problems you see on your job? Explain. _____

_____

_____

UNIT 4

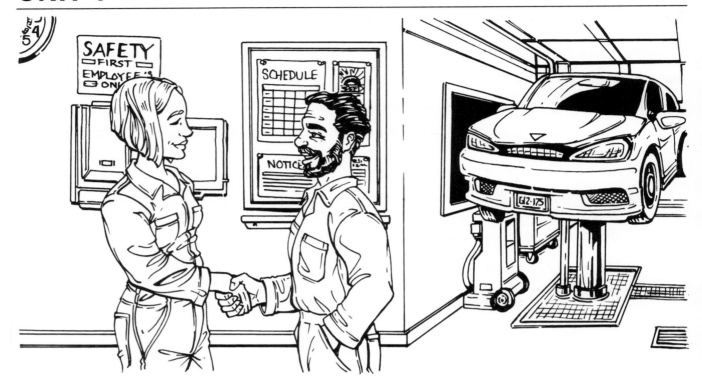

A Schedule Conflict

▶ *Look at the picture. Where do the man and woman work?*

▶ *Read the title. What is a work schedule? What do you think happens in the story?*

1   Rita is an **automotive service technician** at a car dealership. She is **certified** to **inspect**, **maintain**, and **repair** cars. She can **evaluate** car problems. She can **fix** cars.

2   Rita and Sergio work in the service department. They are on the same **work team**. Rita's **shift** is Monday to Friday from 7:30 a.m. to 4:30 p.m. Sergio works Tuesday to Saturday from 7:30 a.m. to 4:30 p.m. Both Rita and Sergio work full time, 40 hours a week.

3   Sergio looks at the work **schedule**. He says, "Rita, can you work next Saturday for me? I need the day off. We're having a **graduation** party for my son."

4   Rita says, "Sure, Sergio. Let's **trade** shifts. You work Monday for me. I'll work Saturday for you." They shake hands.

5   Sergio tells Omar, their supervisor, about the trade. Omar says, "Congratulations, Sergio! Just make sure you come to work on Monday. It is our **busiest** day next week."

6   On Monday morning, the service area is busy. Two technicians are working on cars. Five cars are waiting to be repaired. Omar looks at the clock. It's 7:45 a.m. Sergio is not at work. Sergio is late. Omar is angry.

7   At 8:00 a.m. Omar calls Sergio. "Sergio, where are you? The schedule says you are working today! You were supposed to be here at 7:30 a.m."

8   Sergio says, "Oh no! I overslept. I'm sorry. I'll be there by 9:00 a.m."

9   Omar says, "Sergio, if you ever do this again, you'll be **fired**!"

Check Your Understanding

Answer the questions. Talk with a partner.

1.   What is Rita's job? _____

2.   Name three things Rita is certified to do. _____

3.   According to paragraph 2, what days does Rita usually work? _____

4.   Look at paragraph 2. Does Sergio work the same days as Rita? _____

5.   Why does Sergio need Saturday off? _____

6.   According to the story, what is the busiest day next week? _____

7.   Why is Omar angry? _____

8.   According to paragraph 7, what time does Omar call Sergio? _____

9.   In paragraph _____, Rita and Sergio trade shifts. They shake hands.

10. In paragraph _____, Sergio gives an excuse for being late. He says, "I overslept. I'm sorry."

Story Retell

Number the pictures and sentences in the correct order. Retell the story.

a. _____
Rita and Sergio trade shifts. They shake hands.

d. _____
Sergio looks at the work schedule.

b. _____
Sergio oversleeps. He is late.

e. _____
Rita and Sergio are automotive service technicians at a car dealership.

c. _____
Omar says, "If you ever do this again, you'll be fired!"

Vocabulary Building

Circle the word or phrase that means the same as the vocabulary word(s). Talk about your answers with a partner.

1. She is *certified* to repair cars.

   a. thinking
   b. trained

2. Rita can *evaluate* the problem with a car.

   a. remember
   b. find out

3. Rita's work *shift* is Monday to Friday from 7:30 a.m. to 4:30 p.m.

   a. time
   b. lunch hour

4. The employees *trade* work days.

   a. repair
   b. exchange

5. Monday is the *busiest day* next week.

   a. day with the most customers
   b. slowest day

 ## Talk About Work:
Being Punctual

Practice the dialog with a partner.

Omar: Sergio, you're late.

Sergio: I'm sorry. I didn't hear the alarm clock. I overslept.

Omar: Oversleeping is not an excuse for being late. You're supposed to be here at 7:30 a.m. When you come late, the other technicians have to do your work.

Sergio: It won't happen again, Omar.

Omar: Read the Employee Manual chapter on being **punctual**. If you're late again, you'll lose your job.

Team Talk

Talk with your teammates about being punctual.

- Why does Sergio need to come to work on time?

- Why does Omar want Sergio to read the Employee Manual?

Critical Thinking: Categories

Pairs. Talk about good and bad reasons for being late or missing work. Write your answers in the correct category.

I overslept.	I had a doctor's appointment.
I don't feel well.	My boss is difficult.
I need to finish my school work.	I was hurt yesterday on the job.

Good Reason

1. _____

2. _____

3. _____

Bad Reason

1. _____

2. _____

3. _____

Read About Work: A Work Schedule

Read the work schedule with a partner. Answer the questions.

Work Schedule: Week of April 3–9	Mon.	Tues.	Wed.	Thurs.	Fri.	Sat.	Sun.
Rita	7:30 a.m. – 4:30 p.m.*	7:30 a.m. – 4:30 p.m.*	7:30 a.m. – 4:30 p.m.*	7:30 a.m. – 4:30 p.m.*	7:30 a.m. – 4:30 p.m.*	off	off
Sergio	off	7:30 a.m. – 4:30 p.m.*	7:30 a.m. – 4:30 p.m.*	7:30 a.m. – 4:30 p.m.*	7:30 a.m. – 4:30 p.m.*	7:30 a.m. – 4:30 p.m.*	off
Pete	7:30 a.m. – 4:30 p.m.*	off	12:30 p.m. – 4:30 p.m.	12:30 p.m. – 4:30 p.m.	12:30 p.m. – 4:30 p.m.	7:30 a.m. – 4:30 p.m.*	off
* includes 1-hour lunch break							

1. What days does Rita work? _____

2. What are Rita's days off? _____

3. How long does Rita get for lunch? _____

4. What days does Sergio work? _____

5. What are his days off? _____

6. Who works more hours, Sergio or Pete? _____

Critical Thinking: Problem Solving

Read the problem. Check the good ideas. Write another good idea on the line. Discuss your ideas with your teammates.

Vesna works Monday to Friday from 2 p.m. to 10 p.m. in a furniture factory. She has a seven-year old daughter in school. Vesna needs to talk with her daughter's teacher. The teacher can meet at 3:30 p.m. on Thursday. What can Vesna do?

☐ She can ask her boss for a few hours off.

☐ She can explain her problem to the boss and ask for the day off.

☐ She can call in sick.

☐ She can talk to the teacher on the phone.

☐ She can _____

Workplace Skills Inventory: Good Work Habits

Employers need employees who are good workers. Are you a reliable employee? Are you a responsible employee? Read the work habits listed below. Put a check next to your skills. Circle skills you need to improve.

☐ I am punctual. I come to work on time.

☐ I have good listening skills. I listen to instructions.

☐ I am organized. I organize my work.

☐ I am **responsible**. I work hard.

☐ I have good time management skills. I don't waste time.

☐ I am **reliable**. I finish all my work.

Team Talk and Write

Write about your workplace skills. Then talk with your teammates. Talk about your skills. Talk about areas you need to improve.

I can _____

I need to improve my _____

Internet Research 🔍

Research the types of skills you will need for a job you are interested in. Type "work skills for" and the job title in the search bar. Compare skills you have to the list of skills you need. What skills do you already have? What will you need to learn?

UNIT 5

A Dangerous Decision

▶ *Look at the picture. What is the woman pointing at?*

▶ *Do you think the handyman can help her?*

1   Scott owns a **business**. He is a **handyman**. Scott can fix almost anything. He **repairs** toilets and sinks. He repairs electrical problems.

2   One hot day in August, Monica Alvarez calls Scott. She says, "Scott, my living room window is broken. It has to be **replaced**."

3   Scott comes over to look at the window. He says, "Monica, you need a new window and a new window frame. I'll come back tomorrow. I'll **remove** the old window and window frame and put in a new one."

4   The next day at Monica's house, the weather is hot. Scott puts on **protective clothing**. He wears **safety goggles** to protect his eyes and **gloves** to protect his hands. He **plugs in** the **electric saw** and starts to cut around the window frame. Monica's house is made of **stucco (cement)**. Stucco is hard to cut.

5　　　The sun is very hot. Scott starts to sweat. Scott's safety goggles get **foggy**. He can't see. Scott makes a decision. He decides to **take off** his safety goggles. Scott starts cutting the hard stucco again. Small pieces of stucco fly off the house. One small piece flies into Scott's eye. Scott's eye is red. He is in a lot of pain!

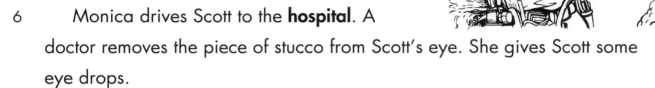

6　　　Monica drives Scott to the **hospital**. A doctor removes the piece of stucco from Scott's eye. She gives Scott some eye drops.

7　　　The doctor tells Scott, "You are very lucky. This could have been much **worse**! Make sure to wear your safety goggles at work. You need to protect your eyes."

Check Your Understanding

Answer the questions. Talk with a partner.

1.　What is Scott's job? _____

2.　Look at paragraph 1. Name two things that Scott can repair. _____

3.　According to the story, is the temperature hot or cold? _____

4.　According to paragraph 4, what protective clothing does Scott wear on the job?

_____

5.　According to the story, Monica's house is made of _____

6.　What machine does Scott use on the job? _____

7.　According to paragraph 5, what decision does Scott make? _____

8.　Why does Scott make that decision? _____

9.　Look at the story again. What does the doctor tell Scott? _____

10.　In paragraph _____, Monica tells Scott she has a broken window.

Story Retell

Number the pictures and sentences in the correct order. Retell the story.

a. _____
A piece of stucco flies into Scott's eye.

d. _____
The weather is hot. Scott puts on safety goggles and gloves.

b. _____
Monica Alvarez calls Scott. She says, "My window is broken."

c. _____
The doctor tells Scott, "Make sure to wear your safety goggles at work."

e. _____
Scott's safety goggles get foggy. He decides to take them off.

Talk About Work: An On-the-Job Injury

Practice the dialog with a partner.

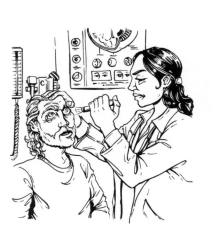

Dr. Singh: Scott, your eye looks red and sore. Tell me what happened.

Scott: I took off my safety goggles while I was working. Now something is in my eye. My eye really hurts.

Dr. Singh: I'm going to numb your eye. Then I'll remove the object.

Scott: OK.

Dr. Singh: Scott, you need to rest your eye for three days. You shouldn't do any work. Put these drops in your eye twice a day.

Scott: I can't work for three days? If I don't work, I won't get paid!

Vocabulary Building

Circle the sentence that means the same. Talk about your answers with a partner.

1. Scott owns a *business*.

   a. He has his own company.
   b. He has a boss.

2. Scott is a *handyman*.

   a. Scott teaches English.
   b. Scott can fix many things.

3. Monica Alvarez asks Scott to *replace* an old window.

   a. She asks Scott to repair the old window.
   b. She asks Scott to put in a new window.

4. Scott puts on *protective clothing*.

   a. He wears goggles to protect his eyes and gloves to protect his hands.
   b. He wears shorts and a T-shirt.

5. Scott puts on *safety goggles* to protect his eyes.

   a. Scott wears regular glasses.
   b. Scott wears special glasses to protect his eyes.

6. He plugs in the *electric saw*.

   a. He connects the saw to electricity.
   b. He uses a hammer.

7. Monica's house is made of *stucco*.

   a. The house is made of metal.
   b. The house is made of cement.

8. Scott's safety goggles get *foggy*.

   a. His glasses are new.
   b. His glasses are covered with drops of water.

9. Scott decides to *take off* his safety goggles.

   a. He puts on protective glasses.
   b. He moves the protective glasses away from his eyes.

10. "This could have been much *worse*!"

   a. You could have been more careful.
   b. You could have been badly hurt.

Critical Thinking: What Did Scott Learn?

Circle the correct answers. Talk about your answers with a partner.

1. a. You need to wear protective clothing at work.

    b. You don't need to wear protective clothing at work.

2. a. You don't need to follow the doctor's instructions.

    b. You need to follow the doctor's instructions.

3. a. It's important to be safe at work.

    b. Safety isn't important.

Talk and Write

Talk with a partner. Write about what Scott should do.

Why does Scott need to go back to work?

_____

What can happen if Scott goes to work before his eye heals?

_____

What do you think Scott should do?

_____

Critical Thinking: Problem Solving

Read the problem. Check the good ideas. Write another good idea on the line. Discuss your ideas with your teammates.

Zoe works in an airplane factory. The machines in Zoe's department are very loud. The sounds from the machines make Zoe's ears ring. What can Zoe do?

☐ Zoe can explain her hearing problem to the **manager**. She can ask for ear plugs.

☐ Zoe can explain the OSHA "no high noise levels" rule to the manager.

☐ Zoe can change departments.

☐ Zoe can look for a different job.

☐ Zoe can _____

Read About Work: OSHA Rules

Read the information about workplace safety below.

Occupational Safety and Health Administration (OSHA)

It doesn't matter if you work in an office, a factory, a hospital, or at a construction site. The U.S. Occupational Safety and Health Administration (OSHA) makes rules to protect all workers. OSHA rules help employers keep workplaces safe and healthy.

OSHA rules protect workers by making sure the place they work is safe.

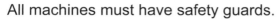

Workplace Safety Rules:

- No dust in the air
- No chemicals that cause illness
- No **fumes**
- No high noise levels
- No electrical or equipment problems

All machines must have safety guards.

All workers must go to safety trainings.

Employers must give workers free protective equipment.

Team Talk

Workplace injury and illness can be *prevented*. Talk with your teammates. What does a safe and healthy workplace look like? What can be done to make a workplace safe?

UNIT 6

A Computer Lesson

▶ *Look at the picture. Where are the people?*

▶ *Read the title. What do you think the teacher is saying to the student?*

1   Pierre works at an **occupational center**. He teaches **computer classes** to adult students. Pierre's students come from all over the world. They are between 18 and 85 years old.

2   Some students in his class have never used a computer. Some students use **electronic devices** like smartphones or tablets. Pierre teaches **basic** computer skills. Students learn skills that are **transferable** to different devices.

3   In Pierre's class, students learn how to use a computer. Students learn to use a **mouse** to **point**, **click**, and **drag**. They learn to **research** information on the **internet**. Students learn to create documents and send **emails**.

4   Pierre tells his students, "This class is like a job." He says, "You need to arrive on time. If you are going to come late, call and leave a message."

5   Pierre tells students, "Come to class prepared. Bring your book, a pen, and a notebook."

6   Students work on group projects in computer class. Pierre says, "In my class, students help each other. They **collaborate**. They work together."

7   One group project is researching (looking up) a word online. Group members divide up the work. They research the information and write a **definition** of the word. They present it to the class.

8   When students finish Pierre's class, they have basic computer skills. They also know how to collaborate on group projects.

Check Your Understanding
Answer the questions. Talk with a partner.

1.   What does Pierre teach? _____

2.   How old are Pierre's students? _____

3.   According to paragraph 2, what are two examples of electronic devices?

_____

4.   According to paragraph 3, what are three ways students use a mouse?

_____

5.   Which other computer skills does Pierre teach? _____

6.   Name three things Pierre tells students to bring to class. _____

7.   What is another way of saying students *collaborate* in a group? _____

8.   Name a research project student groups do in Pierre's class. _____

9.   In paragraph _____, we learn that Pierre's students come from all over the world.

10. What does Pierre mean when he says, "This class is like a job."

_____

Vocabulary Building

Circle the word or phrase that means the same as the vocabulary word(s). Talk about your answers with a partner.

1. He teaches *computer classes* to adult students.

   a. lessons on how to use a computer

   b. lessons on how to sell computers

2. Some students use *electronic devices*.

   a. small computers

   b. heavy equipment

3. Pierre teachers *basic* computer skills.

   a. difficult

   b. easy

4. Students learn skills that are *transferable to different devices*.

   a. can be used on other devices

   b. can only be used on tablets

5. Students *research* information on the internet.

   a. save

   b. look for

6. They send *emails*.

   a. letters in the mail

   b. electronic letters

7. They know how to *collaborate* on group projects.

   a. work alone

   b. work together

Read About Work: Create a Document

Read about how to create a computer document below. Then practice creating your own document.

You can create, save, and print a document on the computer. Follow these simple steps:

Create a New Document

1. Click on the *File* tab in the Main Menu.

2. Click on *New*.

3. Click on *Blank document* and type.

Save a Document

1. On the *File* tab, click *Save As*.

2. Select a *folder* where you will save the document.

3. Type the *File name*. Click *Save*.

Print a Document

1. On the *File* tab, click *Print*.

2. Enter the number of copies you want.

3. Click *Print*.

Talk About Work: Searching the Internet

Practice the dialog with a partner.

Alice: The teacher wants us to research the definition of "computer virus" online. I'm confused. I don't know how. Can you help me?

Sophia: Sure. It's easy. You just need some practice on the internet. First choose a search engine, like Google. Then type "computer virus." After that, press "Enter." The results will appear on the screen.

Alice: That's all? It sounds easy!

Sophia: It is easy. Why don't you practice? Practicing will help you get comfortable with the internet.

Alice: OK. Let's get started!

Critical Thinking: What Did Alice Learn?

Circle the correct answers. Talk about your answers with a partner.

1. a. Doing online research requires you to work step-by-step.

   b. Doing online research requires you to listen to music.

2. a. You don't need to follow instructions.

   b. You need to follow instructions.

3. a. When you search online, results appear on the computer screen.

   b. When you search online, results are sent in the mail.

4. a. Using the internet gets easier with practice.

   b. No practice is necessary.

Role Play: Using a Computer

Practice the dialog with a partner.

> **Student A:** You are helping another person learn to use a computer. You ask:

- Are you sitting close to the desk?

- Are you sitting up straight?

- Are your feet on the floor? Or on a footrest?

- Is the computer screen an arm's length away?

- Is the computer screen directly in front of you?

- Is the top of the computer screen at eye level?

- Are your hands on the keyboard?

- Are you taking a stretch break every 20–30 minutes?

> **Student B:** You are learning to use a computer. You are following the instructions from your partner. You answer the questions.

Team Talk

Talk with your teammates.

- Do you use a computer?

- Do you use the internet?

- What can you do on the computer?

- What would you like to learn to do?

Internet Research

Search for "free basic computer skills training." Locate a site that has free computer tutorials, such as gcflearnfree.org. Watch or read a lesson online. What did you learn?

Critical Thinking: Categories

Check the computer skills. Check the skills you use at school or at work.

		Computer Skills	School or Work Skills
1.	Use the internet to research information.	☐	☐
2.	Send an email.	☐	☐
3.	Be responsible for your work.	☐	☐
4.	Come on time.	☐	☐
5.	Print a document.	☐	☐
6.	Bring a book, a pen, and a notebook to class.	☐	☐
7.	View two documents on the computer at the same time.	☐	☐
8.	Collaborate in a team.	☐	☐
9.	If you are late, call and leave a message.	☐	☐
10.	Click on the mouse.	☐	☐

Talk and Write

Talk with a partner. Write about using computer skills at school and at work.

Why do you need computer skills for work and for school? _____

_____

Which computer skills do you have? _____

_____

_____

Which computer skills do you need to develop? _____

_____

_____

Be Productive!

▶ *Look at the picture. What is the woman doing? What is the man doing?*

▶ *Read the title. What do you think the story is about?*

1   Chen **stocks merchandise** at a **discount store**. She's part of a work team. Today, Chen and her **co-worker**, George, are stocking sheets and blankets in the **home goods** department. They put the merchandise on the shelves.

2   "Do the sheets go next to the blankets?" George asks.

3   "Read the **work order**, George!" Chen says. "Anthony already **warned** me not to talk at work. I can't get into trouble again."

4   George says, "I don't understand the work order."

5   "Put the sheets on the end of the **aisle** where customers can see them," Chen tells George. "We need to make a **display**."

6   Anthony is Chen's boss. He is the team leader. The next day Anthony calls Chen into his office. Anthony says, "Chen, you are talking too much on the job. We talked about this problem one month ago. That was your **warning**. Yesterday, you were talking to George. You were **wasting time**."

7   "I'm sorry, Anthony. I was helping George read the work order. He asked me where to put the sheets."

8   "Chen," Anthony says, "It's your job to read the work order and follow the directions. You need to be more **productive**."

9   "I'm sorry, Chen," Anthony says, but I have to **write you up**. The **write-up** will stay in your file for six months.

Check Your Understanding
Answer the questions. Talk with a partner.

1. Chen and George are part of a work _____

2. George is Chen's co-_____

3. What are Chen and George doing? _____

4. According to paragraph 4, George doesn't understand the _____

5. Is the team leader (Anthony) happy with Chen's work? _____

6. When Anthony talked to Chen one month ago, he gave her a _____

7. The team leader wants Chen to stop talking and be more _____

8. Look at paragraph 9. What does Anthony do? He gives Chen a _____

9. How long will the write-up stay in Chen's file? _____

10. Look at the story again. Do you think Anthony (the boss) should write Chen up? Why or why not? _____

Vocabulary Building

Circle the sentence that means the same. Practice giving work instructions to a partner.

1. Stock the *merchandise*.

   a. Put the items on the shelves.   b. Send the items to customers.

2. Don't *waste time*.

   a. Work slowly and take your time.   b. Work quickly and work hard.

3. Be *productive*.

   a. Do a lot of work.   b. Make a lot of noise while you work.

4. Anthony is the *boss*.

   a. He is part of a work team.   b. He is the team leader.

Critical Thinking: Matching

Match the definition to the correct word or phrase.

_____ 1. home goods   a. written notice of bad work

_____ 2. stock   b. talk to an employee about a work problem

_____ 3. merchandise   c. things used in a home

_____ 4. give a warning   d. group of employees who work together

_____ 5. work order   e. put merchandise on shelves

_____ 6. be productive   f. items for sale

_____ 7. write-up   g. description of a work task

_____ 8. work team   h. work hard

 ## Talk About Work: Getting a Write-Up

Practice the dialog with a partner.

Chen: I am really upset! I just talked to my boss, Anthony. He wrote me up.

Phyllis: I used to work for Anthony. What happened?

Chen: He says I have to stop talking on the job. He says I need to follow the directions on the work order.

Phyllis: Anthony really doesn't want you to talk on the job. You need to read the work order and do what it says. Remember, he's the boss!

Chen: OK, Phyllis. Thanks for your advice.

Workplace Skills Inventory: Teamwork Skills
Check the teamwork skills you have.

- ☐ I collaborate with others.
- ☐ I talk with teammates about problems.
- ☐ I am a productive worker.
- ☐ I do what I say I will do.

- ☐ I like to work on a team.
- ☐ I follow instructions.
- ☐ I listen to my teammates.
- ☐ I can help solve problems.

Team Talk

Employers want to hire productive workers. They want workers with teamwork skills. Look at your workplace skills inventory. Talk about three reasons why an employer would want to hire you.

Read About Work: Restaurant Computers

Read the information about technology and teamwork below.

Technology is the use of computers to solve problems. Technology is always changing the way we do things at work. Here is an example of how work teams adapt to new technology.

In a restaurant, the servers and the chef are part of a work team.

Without technology:

- Servers write food orders on paper. They hand the papers to the chef.

- Servers go to the kitchen to talk to the chef.

With technology:

- Servers place food orders on a computer.

- Servers give instructions to the chef on the computer.

Everyone on the restaurant work team is adapting to the new technology.

Review the Story

Fill in the correct vocabulary words. Read the story with a partner.

Chen and George are _____. They work together on the same work

(classmates, co-workers)

_____. They are reading the _____. Chen explains the work

(team, directions)   (story, work order)

order to George. Their boss, Anthony, says Chen is _____. Anthony wants

(wasting time, warning)

Chen to be more _____. He decides to give Chen a _____.

(productive, cooperation)   (display, write-up)

Chen talks to Phyllis. Phyllis says, "Chen, you have to listen to the boss. You need to read the

work order and _____ the directions."

(follow, talk)

Critical Thinking: Categories

Put these work habits in the correct category.

follow directions	waste time	play games at work
come to work on time	read the newspaper	take long breaks
make personal calls	work together	finish all my work
organize my desk	be productive	leave my desk messy

Good Work Habits

1. _____

2. _____

3. _____

4. _____

5. _____

6. _____

Bad Work Habits

1. _____

2. _____

3. _____

4. _____

5. _____

6. _____

Talk and Write

Talk with a partner. Write about work habits.

What is a good worker? _____

Did your employer ever say you were a productive worker? Explain.

_____

_____

Did you (or someone you know) ever get a write-up at work? What happened?

_____

_____

UNIT 8

Paycheck Problem

▶ *Look at the picture. What does the woman do on her job?*

▶ *Read the title. What is a paycheck? Can you guess what happens?*

1 Neng is a **mail carrier**. She works for the postal service. Neng **delivers** mail to the homes along her **postal route**.

2 Neng works full time. She works five days a week, from Monday to Friday. She works 8 hours a day, 40 hours a week.

3 On weekdays, you can see Neng in her blue **uniform** walking down the street. She carries letters and magazines in a **satchel** on her **shoulder**. First Neng delivers the mail to houses on one side of the street. Then she delivers the mail to houses on the other side. She puts the mail into mailboxes.

4 Neng gets paid every two weeks, on Friday. Neng's total pay after taxes should be $1,500.00. This Friday Neng sees a problem on her paycheck. The total is **wrong**.

5   Neng's paycheck is only $1,125.00 for 60 hours of work. Her check is **short** $375.00! Neng is very **upset**. She needs the money to pay her bills.

6   Neng complains to her supervisor, Ms. Kennedy. Neng says, "I worked 80 hours, not 60! My paycheck is short $375.00."

7   Ms. Kennedy says, "You're right, Neng. It's a mistake. I'm sorry." She fills out a **Payroll Adjustment Form**.

8   The supervisor tells Neng, "In two weeks you'll get your next regular check. In that check you will also get the $375.00."

9   Neng says, "Thanks for your help. I'm glad I looked at my paycheck before I cashed it!"

Check Your Understanding

Answer the questions. Talk with a partner.

1. What is Neng's occupation? _____

2. What does Neng do on her job? _____

3. According to paragraph 2, how many hours a week does Neng work? _____

4. According to paragraph 3, what does Neng carry on her shoulder? _____

5. What does Neng put in her satchel? _____

6. In paragraph 5, why is Neng upset? _____

7. What form does the supervisor fill out? _____

8. When will Neng receive the $375.00? _____

9. In paragraph _____, Neng complains to her supervisor.

10. Why does Neng need to check her paycheck? _____

Story Retell

Number the pictures and sentences in the correct order. Retell the story.

a. _____
Ms. Kennedy fills out a Payroll Adjustment Form.

b. _____
Neng complains to her supervisor, Ms. Kennedy.

c. _____
Neng's paycheck is short $375.00! She is very upset.

d. _____
The supervisor says, "You're right, Neng. It's a mistake. I'm sorry."

e. _____
Neng gets her paycheck on Friday.

Vocabulary Building

Circle the word or phrase that means the same as the vocabulary word(s). Talk about your answers with a partner.

1. Neng *delivers* the mail.
   a. opens it
   b. brings

2. She works *full time*.
   a. 40 hours a week
   b. 15 hours a week

3. When she is working, Neng wears a *uniform*.
   a. protective equipment
   b. special clothes for workers

4. Her paycheck is *short* $375.00.
   a. over
   b. missing

5. Neng looks at her paycheck. She is *upset*.
   a. not happy
   b. happy

Talk About Work: My Paycheck Is Wrong!

Practice the dialog with a partner.

Bobbie: What's wrong, Neng? You look upset.

Neng: I can't believe it! My paycheck is short $375.00. My rent is due tomorrow. And I need to buy groceries.

Bobbie: Tell your landlord what happened. Maybe he'll let you pay part of the rent now, and the other part in two weeks.

Neng: That's a good idea. I'm going to call him.

Team Talk

Talk with your teammates.

- Why does Neng need to call her landlord?

- What may happen if she doesn't pay her rent on time?

- What should Neng do?

- What do you think the landlord will say?

Critical Thinking: Problem Solving

Read the problem. Check the good ideas. Write another good idea on the line. Discuss your ideas with your teammates.

Duane works as a **janitor** at an office building. He works full time, 40 hours a week, on the night shift. He empties the trash. He cleans and polishes the floors. Duane's pay is $11.00 per hour. He is married and has two small children. His pay is not enough for his rent, food, and utilities. What can Duane do?

☐ He can ask his boss for more money.

☐ He can ask to work overtime.

☐ He can try to start his own janitorial business.

☐ He can _____

Read About Work: Reading a Pay Stub

Read the *pay stub* below with a partner. Answer the questions.

PRINCESS CANDY COMPANY

Name Lisa Wright   **Employee Number** 1642   **Hourly Pay** $12.00

Social Security Number 123-45-6789   **Net Pay** $836.61

Pay Period March 4 – March 17, 2018

Pay Type	Rate	Hours	Amount	Deductions	Amount
Regular Pay	12.00	80	960.00	Social Security	65.10
Overtime Pay	18.00	5	90.00	Federal Tax	103.32
				State Tax	20.29
				State Disability Insurance	9.45
				Medicare	15.23
		Total Gross Pay	$1,050.00	**Total Deductions**	$213.39

Questions about the Pay Stub

1. What is the **pay period** on the pay stub? _____

2. According to the pay stub, what is Lisa's hourly pay? _____

3. How many total hours did Lisa work? _____

4. What is Lisa's pay rate for one hour of overtime? _____

5. What is her **gross pay** (before **taxes**)? _____

6. What is her **net pay** (after taxes)? _____

7. How much is **deducted** for federal taxes? _____

8. How much is deducted for state taxes? _____

9. How much is deducted for Social Security? _____

10. How much is deducted for State Disability Insurance? _____

Critical Thinking: Matching

Match the definition to the correct word or phrase.

_____ 1. deduction

_____ 2. gross pay

_____ 3. net pay

_____ 4. taxes

_____ 5. overtime pay

_____ 6. pay period

a. amount you take home after deductions

b. money you pay to the government

c. amount you earn before deductions

d. the days you are paid for

e. pay for working more than 40 hours a week

f. money taken out of a paycheck

Internet Research 🔍

Some jobs pay the minimum wage. That is the lowest pay allowed by law. Some jobs pay more than minimum wage.

Search for "**minimum wage**" on the internet. Fill in the information below, then talk with your teammates. How can you get a good job that pays more than the minimum wage?

1. The federal minimum wage is _____ per hour.

2. The minimum wage in my state is now _____ per hour.

3. The minimum wage in my state will go up on _____ to _____ per hour.

4. Some good jobs that pay higher than minimum wage are: _____

_____

_____

UNIT 9

A Safety Meeting

▶ *Look at the picture. What are the people doing?*

▶ *Read the title. Why are safety meetings at work important?*

1   Jamal and Vlad work at Open Space, a company that makes **screen doors**. Jamal is a **shipping clerk**. Vlad is Jamal's assistant. They work together in the shipping department.

2   On the first Tuesday of every month, Jamal and Vlad go to a **safety meeting**. All employees must attend safety meetings. Safety meetings are **mandatory**.

3   At the safety meetings, employees learn to **prevent** accidents. In today's meeting, they learn safe ways to drive a **forklift**. They learn safe ways to lift boxes using the forklift. They learn to wrap plastic around boxes to prevent injuries.

4   Jamal listens during the safety meeting. He **takes notes**. He writes down the important information. Jamal wants to remember the facts.

5   After the meeting, Jamal and Vlad return to the
shipping department. They **review** their notes. Jamal
and Vlad have work to do. They must follow the safety
instructions they learned.

6   Jamal and Vlad are sending screen doors to
hardware stores. First Vlad puts a **wooden pallet** on
the **warehouse** floor. Next Jamal drives the forklift. He
picks up one box of doors. He sets the box on the wooden pallet. Then Jamal
picks up another box. He **stacks** four boxes on the pallet.

7   The corners of the metal doors are **sharp**. Jamal and Vlad carefully **wrap**
plastic around the boxes. They wrap the boxes from bottom to top. They want
to be sure no one gets hurt. They learned to wrap boxes at the safety meeting.

Check Your Understanding
Answer the questions. Talk with a partner.

1.   Where do Jamal and Vlad work? _____

2.   What is Jamal's job? _____

3.   Look back at the story. What day is the safety meeting? _____

4.   Name two things employees learn at safety meetings. _____

5.   Look at paragraph 4. During the safety meeting, what does Jamal do? He
     _____ and _____.

6.   What does Vlad put on the warehouse floor? _____

7.   Look at paragraph 6. In the warehouse, Jamal drives a _____.

8.   According to the story, what do Jamal and Vlad wrap around the boxes?

     _____

9.   In paragraph _____, Jamal takes notes in a safety meeting.

10. What is another way to say they want to stop injuries? _____

Vocabulary Building

Circle the word or phrase that means the same as the vocabulary word(s). Talk about your answers with a partner.

1. Jamal works at a company that makes *screen doors*.

    a. outside door that lets air in
    b. bedroom door

2. Jamal is a *shipping clerk*.

    a. person who sends products to stores or customers
    b. person who washes clothes in a laundry

3. Every month they go to a *safety meeting*.

    a. a meeting about safety at work
    b. a meeting about ways to relax

4. Safety meetings are *mandatory*.

    a. employees can go if they want to
    b. all employees must go

5. During the safety meeting, Jamal listens and *takes notes*.

    a. draws pictures in his notebook
    b. writes down the main ideas

6. Jamal *stacks* four boxes of doors on the pallet.

    a. puts them on top of each other
    b. puts them on the warehouse floor

7. They *wrap* the boxes with plastic.

    a. cover
    b. carry

In Other Words

Work with a partner. Choose the words that mean the same. Fill in the correct words. Read the new sentences.

1. <u>Jamal and Vlad</u> work together <u>on a team</u>.

    _____ work together _____.
    　　　You, They　　　　　　　　　　　　　　　　*in a group, at a school*

2. <u>Jamal and Vlad</u> <u>wrap</u> the boxes in plastic.

    _____ _____ the boxes in plastic.
    　　　You, They　　　　　　　　*drive, cover*

3. <u>Jamal</u> <u>takes notes</u> at the safety meeting.

    _____ _____ at the safety meeting.
    　　　She, He　　　　　*reads a book, writes down the main ideas*

Talk About Work: Understanding Safety Rules

Practice the dialog with a partner.

Jamal: That was a good meeting! Let's review my notes.

Vlad: I learned a lot! I didn't know that driving fast can make a forklift tip over.

Jamal: You have to drive a forklift slowly. You need to signal first, and turn slowly. You need to slow down on wet and slippery floors.

Vlad: What did they say about honking the horn?

Jamal: They said, "When the load is large, sometimes you can't see around the load. You need to honk to let people know you are coming."

Vlad: I'm glad you took good notes.

Jamal: Me, too. Now let's get back to work!

Critical Thinking: What Did Vlad Learn?
Circle the correct answers.

1. a. You need to follow safety rules.

   b. You don't need to follow safety rules.

2. a. You need to drive a forklift quickly.

   b. You need to drive a forklift slowly.

3. a. When a load is large, you can always see around it.

   b. When a load is large, sometimes you can't see around it.

4. a. Honking the horn lets other people know the forklift is coming.

   b. If you honk the horn, you can drive the forklift faster.

Read About Work: Safety Rules

Read the workplace safety rules below.

SAFETY RULES AT OPEN SPACE

Workplace safety is important. A safe work area saves lives!

- Keep all exits and **aisles** clear. Do not block exits.
- Keep all floors clean and dry.
- Remove all **fire hazards**.
- Wear protective clothing (hats, gloves, goggles) on the job.
- Cover chemicals. Keep all chemicals in safe storage areas.
- Keep ladders, equipment, and machines away from work areas.
- Do a safety check on all forklifts and trucks before driving.

Critical Thinking: Problem Solving

Read the problem. Check the good ideas. Write another good idea on the line. Discuss your ideas with your teammates.

Aviva works on the assembly line in a toy factory. The factory makes plastic children's toys. There are chemical fumes in the factory air. Aviva is afraid she will get sick from the chemical fumes. What can she do?

☐ Aviva can talk to the manager. She can ask for a mask, gloves, and goggles.

☐ Aviva can ask the company to pay for her to see a doctor.

☐ Aviva can report the problem to the company health and safety committee.

☐ Aviva can report the problem to OSHA (Occupational Safety and Health Administration).

☐ Aviva can _____

Team Talk

Talk with your teammates. Why is it important to have a safe work area?

Role Play: Following Safety Rules

Practice the dialog with a partner.

Student A: You are helping the heavy equipment operator check the forklift to be sure it is safe. You ask:

- Do you have your hard hat on?
- Are you wearing safety boots?
- Are your hands clean (free of grease)?
- Does the horn work?

- Did you check the brakes?
- Did you check the seats and mirrors?
- Is the load stable?

Student B: You are the heavy equipment operator. You are checking the forklift to be sure it is safe to drive. You are answering the questions.

Talk and Write

Talk with a partner. Write about a safe workplace.

What is a safe workplace? _____

_____

Why is a safe workplace important? _____

_____

Did you (or someone you know) ever work in a place that was unsafe? Why was it unsafe?

_____

Internet Research

Search for "OSHA workplace safety" and the type of job or workplace you are interested in. Find a list of safety rules. What did you learn?

UNIT 10

A Dose of Medicine

▶ *Look at the picture. What is Mai doing?*

▶ *Read the title. Why is counting pills important?*

1   Mai works in a **pharmacy**. She's a **pharmacy technician**. She helps the **pharmacist**. The pharmacist is her supervisor. "Good **customer service** is number one on my job," Mai says. "The first thing I ask a customer is, 'How can I help you?'"

2   Where did Mai learn customer service? In her pharmacy tech class at school, Mai learned **hard skills**, like dispensing medication. She also learned **soft skills**, like talking to customers.

3   Mai had part of her job interview on the phone. The interviewer asked, "How would you deal with an angry customer?" Mai said, "I'd ask, 'How can I help you?'" She got the job.

4   Mai says, "Pharmacy techs have many **responsibilities**. First we take the customer's **prescription**. We call the insurance company to **verify** insurance. Then we print a medicine **label** and count the pills."

5   Next the pharmacist checks the medication to make sure it is correct. The pharmacist **consults with** customers about taking the medication. They discuss the **dose** (how much medicine to take). They talk about possible **side effects** and **drug interactions**.

6   Before a customer leaves, Mai asks, "Is there anything else I can do for you?" She wants the customer to have a good experience. She wants to be sure the customer comes back.

Check Your Understanding

Answer the questions. Talk with a partner.

1. Where does Mai work? _____

2. What does Mai do? _____

3. According to paragraph 1, who supervises Mai's work? _____

4. Name two kinds of skills Mai learned in her pharmacy tech class at school.

    _____

5. Look at paragraph 2. What is an example of a *soft skill*? _____

6. Look at paragraph 4. Name two of Mai's responsibilities. _____

7. According to paragraph 5, who consults with a customer about taking a medication?

    _____

8. What is the first thing Mai asks a customer? _____

9. What is another word for how much medicine to take? _____

10. Why must the pharmacist check the medication? _____

Vocabulary Building

Circle the word or phrase that means the same as the vocabulary word(s). Talk about your answers with a partner.

1. Mai works in a *pharmacy.*

   a. a store that sells medicine
   b. a store that sells toys

2. To work at a pharmacy, you need good *customer service* skills.

   a. working on a computer
   b. helping customers

3. Mai learned *hard skills* in her pharmacy tech class at school.

   a. skills that you learn with training, like dispensing medication
   b. soft skills, like talking to customers

4. Mai learned *soft skills* in her pharmacy tech class at school.

   a. working with medications
   b. talking to customers

5. Pharmacy techs have many *responsibilities.*

   a. things to do at work
   b. stores that sell medicine

6. She calls the insurance company to *verify* insurance.

   a. check
   b. order

7. She prints a *label* for the medication.

   a. a machine to count pills
   b. paper with information on it

8. The pharmacist *checks* the medication.

   a. makes sure it is correct
   b. works in a pharmacy

9. The pharmacist *consults with* a customer.

   a. talks to
   b. verifies

10. The patient takes *a dose* of medicine.

    a. a label
    b. an amount

Story Retell

Number the pictures and sentences in the correct order. Retell the story.

a. _____

Mai prints a label and counts the pills.

b. _____

The pharmacist checks the medication and consults with the customer.

c. _____

The customer gives Mai a prescription.

d. _____

Mai calls the insurance company to verify insurance.

e. _____

Mai asks the customer, "How can I help you?"

Talk About Work: Reading a Medicine Label

Practice the dialog with a partner.

Juan: When do I take this medicine?

Pharmacist: Take it twice a day for 7 days.

Juan: How much do I take?

Pharmacist: The dose is one pill.

Juan: Do I take it with food?

Pharmacist: Yes, take it with food. Take one pill with breakfast in the morning. Then take another pill with dinner.

Juan: Thank you for helping me understand the directions!

Read About Work: Flu Shots

Read about getting a flu shot at a pharmacy.

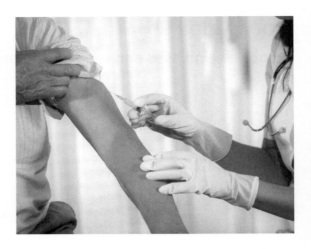

The **flu** (influenza) is a serious illness. The flu is contagious. That means you can give the flu to other people at home, at school, and at work.

People get the flu during flu season. Flu season is October through May. Getting a shot can protect you from getting sick.

The U.S. Centers for Disease Control and Prevention (CDC) recommends that children six months old or older get a flu shot. People age 50 and older should also get the shot. For some people there may be side effects. Some people get a headache, a sore throat, a fever, or muscle aches. Some people may be **allergic** to the medicine. You should not get a flu shot when you are sick with a fever. Check with your doctor to make a good decision.

Where can you get a flu shot? Go to your doctor's office or a pharmacy. When you come in for your shot, wear loose-fitting clothing. Bring your insurance card and photo ID. You need to fill out and sign a form. The form says that you agree to get a flu shot. A pharmacy technician can help you fill out the form.

Review the Readings

Talk with your teammates about the information. Decide if a statement is True (T) or False (F). Write your answer next to the statement.

_____ 1. A pharmacy technician works at a pharmacy.

_____ 2. A pharmacy technician has an easy job. There is a lot of free time.

_____ 3. A pharmacy technician consults with the patient about taking medication.

_____ 4. The pharmacy technician calls the insurance company to verify insurance.

_____ 5. Customer service is not important to a pharmacy technician.

_____ 6. The pharmacist supervises the work of the pharmacy technician.

_____ 7. People age 50 and older should get a flu shot.

_____ 8. The pharmacy technician can help patients fill out the form for a flu shot.

Role Play: At the Pharmacy

Practice the dialog with a partner.

Student A: You are a customer. Your doctor sends a prescription to the pharmacy. You don't feel well. You want your prescription filled right away. You want to get a flu shot. You talk to the pharmacy technician. You ask:

- Can I get my prescription filled now?

- How long do I need to wait?

- When should I come back to get my prescription?

- Can I make an appointment to get a flu shot?

Student B: You are the pharmacy technician. You are trying to help the customer. You have a lot of work. The pharmacist is busy. You are trying to be polite. You say:

- There are a few people ahead of you.

- Can you come back in 30 minutes to pick up your prescription?

- When would you like to come in for your flu shot?

- May I see your insurance card?

Talk and Write About Pharmacy Technician and Pharmacist Jobs

In the United States, the number of pharmacy technician jobs is increasing. Talk with your teammates about pharmacy technician and pharmacist jobs.

Does a pharmacy technician or a pharmacist job interest you?

_____

Where can you find out more about the pharmacy technician or pharmacist jobs in your area?

_____

Get Promoted

▶ *Look at the picture. What is the woman doing?*

▶ *Read the title. What do you think "get promoted" means?*

1   Juanita works in a factory. The factory makes safety harnesses. A **safety harness** prevents a construction worker from falling. A construction worker wears a safety harness to stay safe.

2   Most employees at the factory are **sewing machine operators**. They sew the safety harnesses.

3   Juanita is a **maintenance mechanic**. She repairs broken sewing machines. She replaces parts. Juanita **adjusts** machine settings. Juanita cleans the sewing machines.

4   How did Juanita get her maintenance mechanic job? This was not Juanita's first job in the factory. Before, she was a sewing machine operator. She sewed for twelve years. Then she got a **promotion**!

5   One year ago, her supervisor said, "Juanita, I like your work. I want to **promote** you. We're getting new **computerized** machines. Do you want to learn to fix the new machines?" Juanita said, "Yes!"

6   After that, the company hired a special **trainer** to teach Juanita. Juanita trained on the job. She trained for three months.

7   Juanita learned to **program** the new machines. She learned to replace parts. She learned to clean and **maintain** the machines. She learned to be a maintenance mechanic.

8   Now Juanita is an **experienced** worker. She is good at her job. Her supervisor says, "Juanita's work is excellent." Now Juanita is training another employee to be her **helper**!

Check Your Understanding

Answer the questions. Talk with a partner.

1. Where does Juanita work? _____

2. What does a safety harness do? _____

3. According to paragraph 3, what is Juanita's job? _____

4. Name two things Juanita does as a maintenance mechanic. _____

5. According to paragraph 4, how long did Juanita operate a sewing machine? _____

6. The supervisor said, "Juanita, I like your work. I want to _____ you."

7. According to paragraph 6, who teaches Juanita the new job? _____

8. Where did Juanita train to be a maintenance mechanic? _____

9. In paragraph _____, Juanita is training another employee to be her helper.

10. Look at paragraph 8. What is another way to say Juanita is a skilled worker? _____

Vocabulary Building

Circle the word or phrase that means the same as the vocabulary word(s). Talk with a partner.

1. A safety harness *prevents* a construction worker from falling.

   a. stops   b. makes

2. The factory got new *computerized* machines.

   a. simple   b. run by computers

3. Juanita got a *promotion*.

   a. part-time job   b. better job

4. The company hired a special *trainer* to teach Juanita.

   a. teacher   b. operator

5. Juanita learned to *program* the new machines.

   a. play games on the computer   b. give a computer instructions

6. She *repairs* broken sewing machines.

   a. fixes   b. sews

7. Juanita *adjusts* machine settings.

   a. changes something to work better   b. replaces

8. Juanita is a *maintenance mechanic* in a sewing factory.

   a. sewing machine operator   b. sewing machine repair person

9. She *maintains* the machines.

   a. keeps them in good working condition   b. supervises

10. Juanita is an *experienced* maintenance mechanic.

    a. skilled   b. new

11. She's training another employee to be her *helper*.

    a. assistant   b. teacher

In Other Words

Work with a partner. Choose the words that mean the same. Fill in the correct words. Read the new sentences.

1. A safety harness <u>prevents</u> a worker from falling.

    A safety harness _____ *a worker from falling.*
    makes, stops

2. <u>Juanita</u> started as a sewing machine operator, and then she <u>got promoted</u>.

    _____ *started as a sewing machine operator, and then she* _____.
    She, He   moved down, moved up

3. Juanita is <u>training</u> another <u>employee</u> to be her assistant.

    Juanita is _____ *another* _____ *to be her assistant.*
    teaching, reading   student, worker

Talk About Work: A Performance Evaluation

Practice the dialog with a partner.

Supervisor: Good to see you, Juanita. Are you ready for your **performance evaluation**?

Juanita: Yes, but I'm a little nervous.

Supervisor: Don't worry! We are very happy with your work as a maintenance mechanic. You do a great job fixing the sewing machines. The machine operators are happy with your work, too.

Juanita: Oh, that's good! I really enjoy doing my job. I'm always learning something new.

Supervisor: That's why I'm recommending you for a **pay raise**. It will begin with your next paycheck!

Juanita: That's great! Thank you very much.

Read About Work: Using Technology in Today's Workplace

Computers are everywhere in the workplace. Employers schedule meetings on computers. Restaurant servers send food orders to cooks on computers. Assembly line workers read work orders printed on computers. Factory sewing machines are programmed on computers. Stock clerks read work schedules on smartphones.

Now companies want workers who can use computers. Here are some other work tasks that use computers:

- Send an email

- Read an online work memo

- Keep an online work record

- Read an online work schedule

- Read an online work order

- Punch a time clock

- Keep an online calendar

- Change machine settings

Workplace Skills Inventory: Technology Skills

What technology skills do you have? Can you use a computer at work? Can you use a laptop or a tablet? Can you use a smartphone? What would you like to learn?

I can _____

I can _____

I can _____

I want to learn _____

_____

Review the Story

Fill in the correct vocabulary words. Read the story with a partner.

Juanita is a _____. She works in a factory. She _____
           (cosmetologist, maintenance mechanic)   (repairs, makes)

broken sewing machines. The new machines are _____. In the past, Juanita
                                            (training, computerized)

was a sewing _____ operator. She was _____ from
                  (business, machine)   (happy, promoted)

machine operator to maintenance mechanic.

Critical Thinking: Problem Solving

Check the good ideas. Write another good idea on the line. Discuss your ideas with students in your group.

Ramon works as a stock clerk in a supermarket. He is good at putting the merchandise on the shelves. He is also good at communicating with customers. Ramon wants to be a supermarket manager. What can he do to get a promotion?

☐   Ramon can talk to his boss. He can find out what he needs to learn. He can ask for a promotion.

☐   Ramon can develop his computer skills.

☐   Ramon can read on the internet about getting a promotion.

☐   Ramon can quit his job. He can look for a job at a different company.

☐   Ramon can continue working on his job. He can look for jobs at other supermarkets.

☐   Ramon can _____

Returning to Normal

▶ *Look at the picture. What is the physical therapy aide doing?*

▶ *Read the title. What do you think happened to the patient?*

1   On Annie's job, she helps **injured** patients to move. Today, she is helping a mother. Two weeks ago, the mother was holding her baby. She was walking down the **stairs**. She **twisted** her knee.

2   Annie is a **physical therapy** (PT) **aide**. She works in a **private** clinic. A physical therapist **supervises** Annie's work. Annie helps the woman do some **exercises**. Annie says:

> *Lie on your back.*
>
> *Keep your left knee bent.*
>
> *Keep your right leg straight.*
>
> *Lift the right leg up in the air.*
>
> *Hold for five seconds.*
>
> *Now slowly lower your right leg.*

3   At the clinic, patients learn to do exercises. Exercise helps the body get **stronger**. Exercise strengthens the mother's leg. After working with the physical therapist and Annie for two months, the mother's leg will **heal**. In this clinic, no medicine is **prescribed**. In this clinic, therapists help people's bodies heal naturally.

4   Each patient comes to the clinic with a different problem. Some patients have back problems. Others have arm or leg problems. Every day, the physical therapist talks with Annie about the **requirements** for each patient.

5   Annie says, "The best part of my job is working with patients. When patients come in, they need help. I love helping people return to their **normal** lives."

Check Your Understanding

Answer the questions. Talk with a partner.

1.   What is Annie's job? _____

2.   Where does she work? _____

3.   According to paragraph 1, who is Annie helping today? _____

4.   What happened to the patient? _____

5.   According to paragraph 2, who supervises Annie's work? _____

6.   Look at paragraph 2. What does Annie help the woman do? _____

7.   Look at paragraph 3. Exercise helps the body _____

8.   Look at paragraph 4. What other kinds of problems do patients have in a physical therapy clinic? _____

9.   What does Annie mean when she says, "I love helping people return to their normal lives"? _____

10. Is medicine prescribed by this clinic? Why or why not? _____

Vocabulary Building

Circle the word or phrase that means the same as the vocabulary word. Talk about your answers with a partner.

1. The woman *twisted* her knee.
   a. raised   b. turned

2. A physical therapist *supervises* Annie's work.
   a. grades   b. watches

3. Annie helps the woman do some *exercises*.
   a. physical movements   b. lessons

4. Exercise helps the body get *stronger*.
   a. more relaxed   b. healthier

5. The patient's knee will *heal*.
   a. get better   b. hurt

6. The physical therapist tells Annie about the *requirements* for each patient.
   a. needs   b. bills

7. In this clinic, no medicine is *prescribed*.
   a. ordered by a doctor   b. free

8. I love helping people return to their *normal* lives.
   a. hospital   b. regular, everyday

Critical Thinking: Matching

Match the definition to the correct word or phrase.

_____ 1. steps   a. get better

_____ 2. injured   b. hurt

_____ 3. private   c. regular, everyday

_____ 4. exercises   d. physical movements

_____ 5. heal   e. not public

_____ 6. normal   f. watches

_____ 7. supervises   g. stairs

Talk About Work: Getting Instructions

Practice the dialog with a partner.

Physical Therapist: Here's our plan for Mr. Ramos. First put heat on his back for five minutes. Then have him do some leg lifts.

PT Aide: How many leg lifts?

Physical Therapist: Begin with 10 on each side. After that, let me know how the patient is doing.

PT Aide: OK. I'll check back with you after the leg exercises.

Team Talk:

Talk with your teammates. A physical therapy aide works in a clinic under the supervision of a physical therapist.

- Are you comfortable working under supervision?

- Or do you prefer to work on your own?

Critical Thinking: Problem Solving

Read the problem. Check the good ideas. Write another good idea on the line. Discuss your ideas with your teammates.

Jonas is a physical therapy aide in a clinic. Jonas wants to move up to a better job. In the future, he wants to be either a PT assistant or a physical therapist. He thinks physical therapy school will cost a lot of money. He thinks it will take many years. How can Jonas find out more information?

☐ Jonas can talk to the physical therapist in his clinic. He can find out about jobs, educational requirements, and costs.

☐ Jonas can read about physical therapy schools online.

☐ Jonas can take classes for physical therapy assistant at a community college.

☐ Jonas can talk to a college counselor.

☐ Jonas can _____

Role Play: At the Doctor's Office

Practice the dialog with a partner.

Student A: You are a patient. You have a left shoulder injury. You explain your problem. You show the doctor your injury. You ask the doctor for help.

Student B: You are the doctor. You **examine** the patient. You prescribe physical therapy. You say:

- Can you move your arm?

- Show me where you feel the pain.

- Is it stiff?

- Does it hurt?

- I recommend you go to physical therapy. PT can help you heal so you can use your arm normally.

Read About Work: Physical Therapy

Read about what physical therapists do below.

Partners in Healing

Physical therapists help patients walk and do daily activities. They help people go up and down stairs. They help people get in and out of bed. They help patients move without pain.

Physical therapists use different treatments. They use exercise, heat, cold, massage, water, and electrical stimulation. They do not prescribe medicine. They help the body heal naturally.

Physical therapists collaborate with their patients. They teach patients to do exercises. The exercises help patients to move and heal. Patients do their exercises in the PT office and at home. Patients and therapists are partners in healing.

Team Talk

Talk with your teammates.

- Did you or someone you know ever go to PT?

- What was the medical problem?

- How did PT help the patient to heal?

Talk and Write

Jobs in physical therapy and occupational therapy are increasing. Talk with a partner about the reading: Partners in Healing. Write about therapy jobs.

Does a job in physical therapy or occupational therapy interest you?

_____

_____

How can you find out which kinds of physical therapy jobs (physical therapy aide, physical therapy assistant, physical therapist, occupational therapist) are available in your area?

_____

_____

How can you find about the educational requirements of each job?

_____

Internet Research 🔍

Choose one of the therapy jobs listed above. Research what the therapist does. Make a list of job duties. Research the education and training required for the job.

GLOSSARY

Unit 1: Providing Patient Care
pp. 14–19

activities of daily living – things you do every day, like brushing your teeth, showering, and getting dressed

anatomy – study of the human body

bedridden – can't get out of bed

blood pressure – force that moves blood through the body

caregiver – someone who takes care of another person

certificate – paper that shows your job training

day shift – work time during the day

normal – healthy, regular

on-the-job experience – job practice at work

patients – sick people getting medical care

received – got

register – sign up

small talk – conversation about easy things to talk about

temperature – measure of how warm the body is

vital signs – temperature, blood pressure, or other measures of body functions

wheelchair – chair with wheels to move people

Unit 2: The Customer Is Always Right
pp. 20–25

apologizes – says she/he is sorry

apron – covering that protects your clothes

chef – cook

chokes – gets food stuck in the throat

flavor – taste

manager – supervisor

oven mitt – glove that protects a hand from heat

prepares – cooks

protect – keep safe

protective clothing – clothes that protect the body

regular customer – person who goes to the same business often

restaurant – place to buy and eat food

server – person who brings your food

The customer is always right. – We want to make the customer happy.

wok – metal pan

Unit 3: Be Healthy and Safe at Work
pp. 26–31

bar code – lines that hold information

cashier – person who takes money in a store

complain – say something is wrong

employee – worker

full time – 40 hours a week

hurt – feel pain

Injury Report – written statement of how an injury happened

lose a job – become unemployed

packages – containers

repetitive motion – moving in the same way over and over

repetitive stress injury (RSI) – pain or injury from moving the same way

safety manual – book about staying safe at work

scans – reads a bar code

scanner – machine that reads bar codes

squat down – lower your body by bending the knees

stretch – straighten your arms or legs to make the muscles long

supermarket – large market

take deep breaths – slowly take in a lot of air

twists – turns

wrist – joint where the hand connects to the arm

Unit 4: A Schedule Conflict
pp. 32–37

automotive service technician – person who fixes cars

busiest – having the most to do

certified – trained

evaluate – find out what is wrong with something

fired – lost a job

fix – repair

graduation – ceremony where students get diplomas

inspect – check

maintain – keep in good condition

punctual – on time

reliable – trustworthy

repair – fix

responsible – hardworking

schedule – list of days and times you work

shift – work time

trade – exchange

work team – employees who work together

Unit 5: A Dangerous Decision
pp. 38–43

business – company that buys or sells things

cement – hard material for building

electric saw – power tool that cuts things

foggy – covered with drops of water

fumes – harmful gas or smoke

gloves – coverings for the hands

handyman – person who fixes things

hospital – place where people get medical care

manager – person in charge

plugs in – connects a cord to electricity

prevented – stopped

protective clothing – clothes that protect the body

remove – take out

repairs – fixes

replaced – took away something old and put in something new

safety goggles – glasses to protect the eyes

stucco – cement

take off – remove

worse – more serious

Unit 6: A Computer Lesson
pp. 44–49

basic – easy

click – press a button on a mouse to make something happen on a computer

collaborate – work together

computer classes – lessons on how to use a computer

definition – meaning of a word

drag – move something on a computer using a mouse

electronic devices – small computers

emails – electronic letters sent from one computer to another

internet – system connecting computers around the world

mouse – device that moves the cursor on a computer screen

occupational center – place that helps people train for jobs

point – move a cursor onto something specific

research – look for

transferable – can be used on other devices

Unit 7: Be Productive!
pp. 50–55

aisle – walkway

co-worker – person who works with you

discount store – store that sells items for low prices

display – special way to show items

home goods – things you use at home

merchandise – items for sale

productive – doing more work

stocks – puts items on store shelves

technology – using computers to do things

warned – talked to an employee about a work problem

warning – paper telling a worker to do something (to avoid trouble)

wasting time – not working hard

work order – written description of work to do

write (you) up – tell and document a worker's bad behavior

write-up – written notice of bad work

Unit 8: Paycheck Problem
pp. 56–61

deduction – money taken out of a paycheck

delivers – brings

gross pay – amount you earn before deductions

janitor – person who cleans a building

mail carrier – person who delivers mail

minimum wage – lowest pay allowed by law

net pay – amount you take home after deductions

overtime pay – pay for working more than 40 hours a week

pay period – the days you are paid for

Payroll Adjustment Form – paper to change an employee's pay

pay stub – paper that shows details of a paycheck

postal route – places a mail carrier delivers mail to every day

satchel – bag

short – missing some money

shoulder – where the arm connects to the body

taxes – money you pay to the government

uniform – special clothes for workers

upset – not happy

wrong – not right

Unit 9: A Safety Meeting
pp. 62–67

aisles – walkways

fire hazards – things that can cause a fire

forklift – machine used to lift heavy objects

hardware stores – businesses that sells materials to build and fix things

mandatory – required

prevent – stop

review – talk about

safety meeting – meeting about safety at work

screen doors – outside doors that let air in

sharp – having a pointed edge

shipping clerk – person who sends products to stores or customers

stacks – places items on top of each other

takes notes – writes down the main ideas

warehouse – large building for storing things

wooden pallet – a base to stack things on before lifting

wrap – cover

Unit 10: A Dose of Medicine
pp. 68–73

allergic – having a bad physical reaction to something

consults with – talks to

customer service – helping people who buy a product or service

dose – amount of medicine you take

drug interactions – side effects caused by mixing medications

flu (influenza) – illness with high temperature and body aches

hard skills – skills that you learn with training, like dispensing medications

label – paper with information on it

pharmacist – person who prepares prescriptions

pharmacy – store that sells medicine

pharmacy technician – person who helps a pharmacist

prescription – written order for medicine from a doctor

responsibilities – things you need to do at work

side effects – possible reactions to a medication

soft skills – personal skills, like talking to customers

verify – check

Unit 11: Get Promoted
pp. 74–79

adjusts – changes something to work better

computerized – run by a computer

experienced – skilled

helper – assistant

maintain – keep in good working condition

maintenance mechanic – person who repairs machines

pay raise – pay increase

performance evaluation – supervisor reviews an employee's work

program – give a computer instructions

promote – move to a higher position at work

promotion – better job

safety harness – belt worn on the body to prevent falling

sewing machine operators – people who use sewing machines

trainer – teacher

Unit 12: Returning to Normal
pp. 80–85

examine – look at

exercises – physical movements

heal – get better

injured – hurt

normal – regular, everyday

physical therapy (PT) aide – person who helps a physical therapist

prescribed – ordered by a doctor

private – not public

requirements – needs

stairs – steps

stronger – healthier

supervises – watches

twisted – turned

ANSWER KEY

Unit 1: Providing Patient Care
Check Your Understanding, p. 15
1. Joy works the day shift in a hospital.
2. She is a Certified Nursing Assistant.
3. According to paragraph 1, activities of daily living include: getting out of bed, going to the bathroom, brushing teeth, taking a shower, getting dressed, and eating.
4. According to paragraph 3, in the Personal Care Assistant class, Joy learned about hand washing, lifting and turning a bedridden patient, moving a patient to a wheelchair, and making small talk.
5. "You look nice today," is an example of small talk.
6. According to paragraph 5, vital signs are blood pressure and temperature.
7. She learned anatomy.
8. Joy took a written test and a patient care test.
9. In paragraph 6, Joy received a CNA certificate from her state.
10. Joy asks patients, "Are you dizzy?" to see how they are feeling.

Vocabulary Building, p. 16
1. a   3. a   5. a
2. b   4. b

In Other Words, p. 16
1. They go to work in the morning.
2. She got work practice in a nursing home.
3. Joy helps sick people and takes their vital signs.

Read About Work, p. 18
1. Date of Birth: July 30, 1990
2. Doctor: Dr. David Suttles
3. The normal blood pressure range is 120/80.
4. The patient's blood pressure is 140/90.
5. No, the patient's blood pressure is higher than normal.

Unit 2: The Customer is Always Right
Check Your Understanding, p. 21
1. Eddie Chan is a chef.
2. According to paragraph 1, he works in a Chinese restaurant.
3. He stands in front of a hot stove. He prepares food in a wok.
4. "Wok" is another word for "pan."
5. Eddie wears an apron to protect his body and an oven mitt to protect his hand.
6. According to paragraph 2, the customer orders garlic shrimp.
7. According to paragraph 6, Mr. Millman is unhappy with his food because it is too salty.
8. The restaurant's rule is, "The customer is always right!"
9. In paragraph 8, the manager apologizes.
10. In paragraph 5, the customer chokes on his shrimp.

Story Retell, p. 22
a. 4   c. 3   e. 2
b. 1   d. 5

Vocabulary Building, p. 22
1. a   3. b   5. a
2. b   4. a

Critical Thinking: What Did Eddie Learn?, p. 23
1. a   3. a
2. b   4. b

In Other Words, p. 24
1. Every day he cooks food in a pan.
2. The server says, "The customer is not happy with his food."

Unit 3: Be Healthy and Safe at Work
Check Your Understanding, p. 27

1. Maria is a cashier at Fresh Foods Market.
2. According to the story, she works full time.
3. Maria uses a scanner at work every day.
4. The scanner reads the bar code on each item.
5. According to paragraph 2, Maria picks up items and moves them across the scanner window. Sometimes she turns the packages to find the bar code.
6. According to paragraph 3, she twists her wrist to scan the code.
7. *Repetitive motion* is in paragraph 4.
8. Maria's hands and wrists hurt because she moves items across the scanner every day.
9. Paragraph 2 tells what the scanner does.
10. In paragraph 6, Julio tells Maria to talk to her boss about the problem.

Vocabulary Building, p. 28

1. b   3. a   5. b
2. a   4. b

Employee Injury Report, p. 29

Employee name: Maria Gonzalez

Job title: Cashier

Date and time of injury: Every day

Describe the injury: My hands and wrists hurt.

Describe what happened and where: It hurts every time I use the scanner.

In Other Words, p. 29

1. Maria works at a large market. She uses a machine that reads bar codes every day.
2. Maria turns the containers to find the bar code.
3. The pain in her wrists can increase.

Unit 4: A Schedule Conflict
Check Your Understanding, p. 33

1. Rita is an automotive service technician.
2. Rita is certified to inspect, maintain, and repair cars.

3. According to paragraph 2, Rita works from Monday to Friday.
4. No, according to paragraph 2, Sergio works Tuesday to Saturday.
5. Sergio needs Saturday off because he is having a graduation party for his son.
6. According to the story, Monday is the busiest day next week.
7. Omar is angry because Sergio is not at work.
8. According to paragraph 7, Omar calls Sergio at 8:00 a.m.
9. In paragraph 4, Rita and Sergio agree to trade shifts. They shake hands.
10. In paragraph 8, Sergio gives an excuse for being late. He says, "I overslept. I'm sorry."

Story Retell, p. 34

a. 3   c. 5   e. 1
b. 4   d. 2

Vocabulary Building, p. 34

1. b   3. a   5. a
2. b   4. b

Critical Thinking: Categories, p. 35
Good Reason

1. I don't feel well.
2. I had a doctor's appointment.
3. I was hurt yesterday on the job.

Bad Reason

1. I overslept.
2. I need to finish my school work.
3. My boss is difficult.

Read About Work: A Work Schedule, p. 36

1. Rita works from Monday to Friday.
2. Rita is off on Saturday and Sunday.
3. Rita gets one hour for lunch.
4. Sergio works from Tuesday to Saturday.
5. Sergio is off Sunday and Monday.
6. Sergio works more hours than Pete.

Unit 5: A Dangerous Decision
Check Your Understanding, p. 39
1. Scott is a handyman.
2. According to paragraph 1, Scott can fix toilets and sinks. He repairs electrical problems.
3. According to the story, the temperature is hot.
4. According to paragraph 4, Scott wears safety goggles and gloves.
5. According to the story, Monica's house is made of stucco (cement).
6. Scott uses an electric saw on the job.
7. According to paragraph 5, Scott decides to take off his safety goggles.
8. Scott starts to sweat and his goggles get foggy.
9. The doctor tells Scott, "You are lucky. This could have been much worse. Make sure to wear your safety goggles at work. You need to protect your eyes."
10. In paragraph 2, Monica tells Scott she has a broken window.

Story Retell, p. 40
a. 4   c. 5   e. 3
b. 1   d. 2

Vocabulary Building, p. 41
1. a   5. b   9. b
2. b   6. a   10. b
3. b   7. b
4. a   8. b

Critical Thinking: What Did Scott Learn?, p. 42
1. a   2. b   3. a

Unit 6: A Computer Lesson
Check Your Understanding, p. 45
1. Pierre teaches computer classes.
2. His students are between 18 and 85 years old.
3. According to paragraph 2, two examples of electronic devices are smartphones and tablets.
4. According to paragraph 3, students use a mouse to point, click, and drag.
5. Pierre teaches students to research information on the internet, to create and print documents, and to send emails.
6. Pierre tells students to bring a book, a pen, and a notebook to class.
7. Students work together. They help each other.
8. Students look up the definition of a word online. They present the definition to the class.
9. In paragraph 1, we learn that Pierre's students come from all over the world.
10. Pierre means that the class is work. Students need to come to class on time. Students need to be prepared to work.

Vocabulary Building, p. 46
1. a   4. a   7. b
2. a   5. b
3. b   6. b

Critical Thinking: What Did Alice Learn?, p. 47
1. a   3. a
2. b   4. a

Unit 7: Be Productive!
Check Your Understanding, p. 51
1. Chen and George are part of a work team.
2. George is Chen's co-worker.
3. Chen and George are stocking sheets and blankets.
4. According to paragraph 4, George doesn't understand the work order.
5. No. Anthony is not happy with Chen's work.
6. One month ago, Anthony gave Chen a warning.
7. The team leader wants Chen to stop talking and be more productive.
8. In paragraph 9, Anthony gives Chen a write-up.
9. The write-up will stay in Chen's file for six months.
10. Answers may vary.

Vocabulary Building, p. 52

1. a
2. b
3. a
4. b

Critical Thinking: Matching, p. 52

1. c
2. e
3. f
4. b
5. g
6. h
7. a
8. d

Review the Story, p. 54

Chen and George are co-workers. They work together on the same work team. They are reading the work order. Chen explains the work order to George. Their boss, Anthony, says Chen is wasting time. Anthony wants Chen to be more productive. He decides to give Chen a write-up. Chen talks to Phyllis. Phyllis says, "Chen, you have to listen to the boss. You need to read the work order and follow the directions."

Critical Thinking: Categories, p. 55

Good Work Habits

1. follow directions
2. come to work on time
3. organize my desk
4. work together
5. be productive
6. finish all my work

Bad Work Habits

1. make personal calls
2. waste time
3. read the newspaper
4. play games at work
5. take long breaks
6. leave my desk messy

Unit 8: Paycheck Problem

Check Your Understanding, p. 57

1. Neng is a mail carrier.
2. She delivers mail to homes along her postal route.
3. According to paragraph 2, Neng works 40 hours a week.
4. According to paragraph 3, Neng carries a satchel on her shoulder.
5. She puts letters and magazines in her satchel.
6. Neng is upset because her paycheck is short $375.00.
7. The supervisor fills out a Payroll Adjustment Form.
8. Neng will receive the $375.00 in two weeks.
9. In paragraph 5, Neng complains to her supervisor.
10. She checks her paycheck to make sure it is correct.

Story Retell, p. 58

a. 5
b. 3
c. 2
d. 4
e. 1

Vocabulary Building, p. 58

1. b
2. a
3. b
4. b
5. a

Questions about the Pay Stub, p. 60

1. March 4–17, 2018
2. $12.00
3. 85 hours
4. $18.00
5. $1,050.00
6. $836.61
7. $103.32
8. $20.29
9. $65.10
10. $9.45

Critical Thinking: Matching, p. 61

1. f
2. c
3. a
4. b
5. e
6. d

Unit 9: A Safety Meeting

Check Your Understanding, p. 63

1. Jamal and Vlad work at Open Space, a screen door company.
2. Jamal is a shipping clerk.
3. The safety meeting is on the first Tuesday of every month.

4. At safety meetings, employees learn to prevent accidents. They learn safe ways to drive a forklift. They learn to wrap plastic around boxes to prevent injuries.

5. He <u>listens</u> and <u>takes notes</u>.

6. Vlad puts a wooden pallet on the warehouse floor.

7. In the warehouse, Jamal drives a <u>forklift</u>.

8. According to the story, Jamal and Vlad wrap plastic around the boxes.

9. In paragraph <u>4</u>, Jamal takes notes in a safety meeting.

10. They want to be sure no one gets hurt.

Vocabulary Building, p. 64

1. a	4. b	7. a
2. a	5. b	
3. a	6. a	

In Other Words, p. 64

1. <u>They</u> work together <u>in a group</u>.

2. <u>They</u> <u>cover</u> the boxes in plastic.

3. <u>He</u> <u>writes down the main ideas</u> at the safety meeting.

Critical Thinking: What Did Vlad Learn?, p. 65

1. a	3. b
2. b	4. a

Unit 10: A Dose of Medicine
Check Your Understanding, p. 69

1. Mai works in a pharmacy.

2. She is a pharmacy technician.

3. According to paragraph 1, the pharmacist supervises Mai's work.

4. Mai learned hard skills and soft skills in her pharmacy tech class at school.

5. According to paragraph 2, one soft skill is talking to customers.

6. According to paragraph 4, Mai's responsibilities include: taking the prescription, verifying insurance, labeling the medicine, and counting the pills.

7. According to paragraph 5, the pharmacist consults with a customer about taking medication.

8. The first thing Mai asks a customer is, "How can I help you?"

9. *Dose* is another word for how much medicine to take.

10. The pharmacist must check the medication to make sure it is correct.

Vocabulary Building, p. 70

1. a	5. a	9. a
2. b	6. a	10. b
3. a	7. b	
4. b	8. a	

Story Retell, p. 71

a. 4	c. 2	e. 1
b. 5	d. 3	

Review the Readings, p. 72

1. T	4. T	7. T
2. F	5. F	8. T
3. F	6. T	

Unit 11: Get Promoted!
Check Your Understanding, p. 75

1. Juanita works in a factory that makes safety harnesses.

2. A safety harness prevents a construction worker from falling.

3. According to paragraph 3, Juanita is a maintenance mechanic.

4. Juanita repairs broken sewing machines. She replaces parts.

5. According to paragraph 4, she sewed for 12 years.

6. The supervisor said, "I like your work. I want to <u>promote</u> you."

7. According to paragraph 6, a special trainer teaches Juanita the new job.

8. According to the story, Juanita trained on the job.

9. In paragraph 8, Juanita is training another employee to be her helper.

10. According to paragraph 8, Juanita is an experienced worker.

Vocabulary Building, p. 76

1. a	5. b	9. a
2. b	6. a	10. a
3. b	7. a	11. a
4. a	8. b	

In Other Words, p. 77

1. A safety harness <u>stops</u> a worker from falling.
2. <u>She</u> started as a sewing machine operator, and then she <u>moved up</u>.
3. Juanita is <u>teaching</u> another <u>worker</u> to be her assistant.

Review the Story, p. 79

Juanita is a <u>maintenance mechanic</u>. She works in a factory. She <u>repairs</u> broken sewing machines. The new machines are <u>computerized</u>. In the past, Juanita was a sewing <u>machine</u> operator. She was <u>promoted</u> from machine operator to maintenance mechanic.

Unit 12: Returning to Normal
Check Your Understanding, p. 81

1. Annie is a physical therapy aide.
2. She works in a private clinic.
3. According to paragraph 1, Annie is helping a mother.
4. The patient twisted her knee.
5. According to paragraph 2, a physical therapist supervises Annie's work.
6. Annie helps her do exercises.
7. Exercise helps the body <u>get stronger</u>.
8. According to paragraph 4, patients in a physical therapy clinic can have problems with their back, legs, or arms.
9. She means she likes to help people to heal and move on their own.
10. No medicine is prescribed by the clinic. Physical therapists help people heal their bodies naturally.

Vocabulary Building, p. 82

1. b	4. b	7. a
2. b	5. a	8. b
3. a	6. a	

Critical Thinking: Matching, p. 82

1. g	4. d	7. f
2. b	5. a	
3. e	6. c	